Love your Challenges

Seven Success habits to Achieve your life's Mastery

DR. PRIANK GUPTA

 A catalogue record for this book is available from the National Library of Australia

Copyright © 2019 Dr. Priank Gupta

All rights reserved.

This publication is copyright. No part of this book may be reproduced, stored in any retrieval system, or transmitted, in any form or by any means without the prior written permission of the copyright owner. Inquiries should be addressed to the publishers.

Disclaimer: The views and opinions expressed in this book are those of the author, based on his personal experiences in life and business, and the book is intended to provide inspirational and valuable general guidance, however, readers must consider their own circumstances before accepting the opinions of the author and applying them in their own circumstances. The author makes no representation as to the suitability or validity of the content of this book to the personal circumstances of the individual who will read the book and will not be liable for any errors, omissions, loss, damage or claims arising from the contents of this book. The author is immensely grateful to the governing laws of AHPRA, all the legal authorities involved in his personal case and the complainant. His personal story is only meant as an inspirational tool for the wider society and should not be considered as a means to tarnish the image of any parties involved.

Publisher:
ASPG (Australian Self Publishing Group)
P.O. Box 159, Calwell, ACT Australia 2905
Email: publishaspg@gmail.com
http://www.inspiringpublishers.com

National Library of Australia Cataloguing-in-Publication entry

Author: Dr. Priank Gupta

Title: **Love your Challenges**/*Dr. Priank Gupta*

ISBN 978-1-925908-86-2 (pbk)

This book is dedicated to all my readers, clients and audiences. Being a general practitioner, I am aware of the problems faced by you in your daily life. This book is written with a mindset to love and embrace your obstacles and challenges. Hence, in a way, this book is dedicated to the hardships and adversities faced by you every day. I have a firm conviction that these significant challenges have a tremendous power to transform your life.

With immense gratitude
Dr Priank Gupta

This book is a must-read. It helps you discover the mastery of your life by embracing your challenges. The MASTERS framework designed by Dr. Priank is simple, practical and highly motivating. I enjoyed the short stories section which helps us achieve a state of peak potential.

Sam cawthorn
Resilience Coach, Keynote speaker, and
CEO Speakers institute

This book will change your life. Dr Priank Gupta has put together a collection of stories that will directly relate to you on some level. If you are challenged, going through a tough time or want to make the most out of life; and let's face it, we all are at some point, this book is for you. Enjoy!

Jodie Spiteri-James
Global Programs Director
Speakers Institute

About the Author

Dr. Priank Gupta is a practicing general practitioner (GP) in Australia. He enjoys working with his wife in a family-run practice in Wollongong and is passionate about general practice and the huge impact it has on the community. He regularly teaches medical students and mentors GP registrars, who themselves are the GPs of future generations. His mission in life is to serve underprivileged children and empower women in the third world and developing countries. He contributes to the Ekal Vidyalaya Foundation (schools run by one teacher), a non-profit organization involved in education and village development in rural and tribal villages of India. He is guided by his mission to write books which bring out the best in all of us, as well as a commitment to becoming a powerful speaker and influencer. He is very clear that a significant proportion of the financial profits gained through these activities will be channeled towards his mission.

In his spare time, he loves playing ping-pong with his son and takes the utmost care with guiding his kids to becoming better citizens of the world. He has run a marathon with the aim of raising funds for a hospice charity in the UK. Dr. Gupta has lived in 3 continents over 3 decades and the thousands of interactions he has had with his clients have shaped him profoundly.

Being a GP means he engages with clients from diverse backgrounds and unique situations. This has made him more grounded, aware of the challenges a common man faces in everyday life, and a more active citizen of the global community. He firmly believes that true wisdom occurs when we take a step in the right direction of our true calling and purpose in life.

When an old door slams with a bang,
A new window opens with a song.
Softly... gently... quietly...yet instantly,
So, wake up, my dear friends,
There are seeds of opportunity in every adversity.
Seize it,
Adore it,
Conquer your challenges,
Accept the hard times,
Because that's how you grow.
Love your Challenges.

Contents

1. A note to you, My Readers 11
2. Love Your Challenges - part 1 17
3. Love Your Big Challenges - part 2 20
4. Science and Art of Happiness. 34
5. Story of Big Rocks, Pebbles, Sand and Water 39
6. What do we stand for? What is Your Story? 42
7. Story of Importance versus Urgency 45
8. Story of Gratefulness 50
9. Story of Empowering Girls 52
10. Story of Marathon of Hope 55
11. Story of Purpose of life 59
12. Story of Kindness and Respect 62
13. Story of Quality and Quantity Time 64
14. Story of staying Cocooned in our Comfort Zones ... 66
15. Story of a Champion Mindset 69
16. Story of Our Response to Challenges 73

17. Story of Appreciation 77
18. Story of Stress 79
19. Story of Happiness 82
20. Story of Forgiveness and Acceptance 85
21. Story of Heart 88
22. Story of Growing Fire in Your Belly 91
23. Story of beginning with the end in mind.
    Enjoy the Ride. 94
24. Introduction to MASTERS 96
25. Mindfulness and Meditation 100
26. Affirmations 104
27. Smile and Silence 108
28. Think and Thank 117
29. Exercise 124
30. Reading 129
31. Story Sharing and Scribble 134
32. Practicing MASTERS in daily life 143
33. Final thoughts on MASTERS 147
34. References 148
35. Acknowledgments 151

A note to you, my readers

Love your challenges? What? Really? These are three questions that may have popped into your mind. I would have had exactly the same response about 5 years ago. I have grown since then and I give all the credit to the challenges I have experienced, especially in the last few years of my life.

Happiness and collective teamwork are crucial for our growth; it creates a peaceful atmosphere and a shield around us and our loved ones. Today's modern world is full of distractions. In this fast-paced, frantic world, it is a daunting task to reflect, introspect, and have a vision. Time is the most precious commodity, but most of us just don't have it. This lack of time is not aided by the array of technology that surrounds our daily lives. In fact, the average human attention span has reduced to just 7 seconds. Although technology can be a wonderful servant, it must stay as a servant and no more. How we utilize this tool depends on our principles and values, as well as our broader vision.

It is therefore vital to ask ourselves the following important questions:

1. What values do we have?
2. What principles do we wish to follow?
3. What is the meaning and purpose of our lives?
4. What is the most important thing to us?

> "The unexamined life is not worth living."
>
> — *Socrates*

What does it mean?

If we have not examined our lives - our core values, the principles we stand for, our goals, dreams and aspirations, and the greater purpose of our life - then we are not really living worthy lives. We are just floating through life without adding any richness or meaning. On our deathbed, or during the latter stages of our lives (which we humans are quite adept at prolonging), we may have more regrets than happy memories. But this is only if we are just passing through life. If we do exactly the opposite, we will live rich and meaningful lives in which our collaborative contribution is prolific, highly influential and positive.

The process of examining our lives, in reality, is a life-changing phenomenon in itself. It involves deep reflection, introspection, silence, meditation, visualization, reading and listening to great books, and journaling our thoughts. Mornings are great. They are a peaceful time of day when we can cultivate these habits. It is relatively easier for early birds; however, anyone can do this with patience and perseverance, at times which suit them better. In answering these questions, we should consider two important concepts:

1. Pleasure (moment to moment happiness)
2. Purpose (sustained, lasting bliss)

Pleasure is a feeling that facilitates happiness in the moment; for example, enjoying a warm barista-made coffee, having a warm shower or bath, a leisurely drive in our favorite car, or simply good times with our families and friends.

Purpose is a concept that is much deeper. This brings us enduring, sustained happiness. Its effect lasts much longer, making us feel proud, accomplished and motivated. Any action that helps others in a positive manner is purposeful, and the more appealing the cause, the stronger the degree of happiness. For instance, helping a charity is meaningful and has a purpose. It doesn't matter if we donate a little or a lot; but the fact that we contribute consistently is more important.

I have read and listened to hundreds of inspiring self-help books over the last 25 years, and exposure to medical school and postgraduate university has also influenced me greatly. However, the most fruitful learning experience I gained (and continue to gain) is working as a GP (general practitioner). This direct human interaction taught me about the challenges people face everyday and I now have a huge appreciation for human strength and endurance. The scientific concept of neuroplasticity has also broadened our tunneled vision. Simply put, it means that all humans, and all living beings (other animals and plants) have a huge capacity to mold themselves and adapt for survival and evolution. We should learn from our past mistakes, but this should not affect our present or future. In fact, we should be actively seeking bolder projects and challenges for the sake of our own worth and purpose. This is most directly linked with our sustained happiness levels.

Finally, as it was once so eloquently put, "Happiness is a journey, not the destination. So, relish it, enjoy to the fullest and make all your smiles count." Nowadays, I listen to audiobooks on the go during my commute to help me broaden my understanding of the world, my vision and to get some unique perspectives.

This book is a collection of 21 timeless principles, in the form of short stories that we should actively consider in life, reflecting and making changes as we progress. I have chosen this form to engage my readers, with true stories to inspire and fables to express my views creatively.

It is not just a book to be read.
It is a book from which you can take action.
Our philosophy in life is simple, yet powerful.
Simplicity is simple yet not easy.
It requires consistent action and a persevering mindset for growth.
Dream Big,
Start Small,
Act now.
Starting a project is a bold step,
And boldness makes us brave.
Let's dive in...

This book is divided into 3 sections. There are 21 stories in the first 2 sections. The third section comprises seven habits to help us become MASTERS of our own DESTINY. When I started writing this book, I incorporated stories and principles which influenced me profoundly. A few months into writing, I realized it would be incomplete if I excluded my own story. Hence, I started writing it, encapsulating the most important principles. The main reason was to share:

1. My own vulnerability, mistakes, failures and challenges, detailing how struggles are part and parcel of everyone's lives. We all have emotions which make us uniquely human.
2. How we can transform stumbling blocks into stepping stones.

You (my beloved readers) can either take the conventional path and read from the beginning to the end - which is great. That way, you will get my story first (and therefore, get to know the author), then read all other stories, culminating in the MASTERS habit. The next option is to dive in stories in whichever way you like and finish them all before moving to MASTERS. The option of diving directly into MASTERS is enticing but may not be very helpful. The scientific rationale of reading the stories first is to cultivate a mindset and become so inspired that the passion of practicing the MASTERS habit becomes rooted, deep within your belly. It is a simple, yet powerful framework.

No more rules now.

Let's begin...

To laugh often and much;
to win the respect of intelligent people
and the affection of children;

to earn the appreciation of honest critics
and endure the betrayal of false friends;
to appreciate beauty,

to find the best in others;
to leave the world a bit better,
whether by a healthy child,

a garden patch, or a redeemed social condition;
to know even one life has breathed easier
because you have lived.

This is the meaning of success.

— Ralph Waldo Emerson

Love your challenges

Hi. My name is Priank and although I live in a major city in Australia now, I spent my childhood years in a small city Moradabad, four hours' drive from New Delhi, India. My parents bonded via a traditional arranged marriage, which is still quite a common custom in India. During my childhood, I was extremely shy and introverted, which meant books were some of my best friends.

I joined the medical school at Allahabad University, India at age 18. There, I met the love of my life, Priyanka. Since our names were so similar, our biochemistry teacher intentionally called me Priyanka and my future wife Priyank during the class roll calls. This would instantly bring an atmosphere of laughter and happiness among all students, and for many months, this elevated my shyness.

There are many events in life which are destined to happen, and I was no exception to this rule. It turned out that Priyanka lived at the next train station to my hometown, which meant that I could spend more time with her on our train journeys back home. I quickly discovered other commonalities between us; our dates of birth, our sun signs and several others. I convinced myself that we were made for each other. In love, I failed to recognize the differences between our families; for example, caste. (The caste system divides Hindus into four main categories - Brahmins (priests and teachers), Kshatriyas (rulers and warriors), Vaishyas (merchants and traders) and the Shudras (laborers)).

I proposed to her in the first year of medical school and she accepted. I was over the moon and we were very happy. My tendency to be a loner slowly dissipated after that. We passed our internships together and successfully pursued master's degrees in Surgery from Agra, India. My next big challenge was to get my parents to meet Priyanka and, more importantly, like her. It was an arduous task for me to accomplish as I was the very first one in my extended family to break the customary tradition of arranged marriage and marry the girl I love. Also, there were significant differences in our families' culture and traditions. Needless to say, I was met with strong opposition from both our sets of parents, which lasted for a few years before they finally agreed, and we married at age 25. Our daughter was born 2 years later, and we were ecstatic.

I was planning to do a post-doctorate degree after completing my Master's, but mother nature and destiny had her own grand plans. Instead, we moved to the UK with hopes of going through higher education there. There were significant challenges from my family, as my parents were not happy seeing me leaving India. We overcame emotional obstacles amongst all the other tribulations of relocating to a foreign country; especially when we had a young family to cater for.

We finally passed our entrance exams for general practice in North Wales, UK. It was a dream come true and we felt invincible, as we were able to buy our first home with a mortgage. The next 6 years passed fairly quickly, as we moved up our respective career ladders and were practicing full-time general practice. I also passed through various stages of working as a casual doctor (locum), a salaried doctor and finally working as a self-employed general practitioner. Our son was born during that time and we were all very happy.

At the same time though, I was becoming both physically and mentally exhausted and burnt out due to working full time and not being able to devote enough time to my wife and kids. The National Health Service (NHS) in the UK was also becoming quite a challenging environment to work in, and there was little help from the higher authorities. We finally made a life-changing decision to move to the other side of the world - Australia, a country of fresh hopes, desires and ambitions. Over the following 12 months, we were finally able to immigrate to our dream country.

I usually only share this story with my very close friends. Now, I believe the time has arrived to remove the mask of introversion and go beyond myself. The main purpose of sharing this story is to make you understand me better. I have now summarized the major challenges experienced in the first half of my life. I believe that, although my story may be completely different to yours, the underlying emotions experienced will remain quite relatable for you.

Love your Big Challenges

So, here we are. At age 40, both of us were working full time in an urban medical center in Wollongong, about an hour away from Sydney. When we came to Australia, we made up our minds never to be self-employed (a fixed mindset), as we thought there were so many responsibilities, and little pay off. So, we decided to work for someone else - a non-medical owner with a group of doctors. We were exposed to one of the most disturbing environments in any organization- political backbiting and financial matters with peers. Things were going from bad to worse.

One Friday afternoon, I got a call from my senior colleague, advising me that another colleague had made an official complaint about me to the higher authorities. In fact, it wasn't just a couple of matters, rather a total of 10 complaints. I had been sensing the tension in the few weeks leading up to this. Honestly, though, there was only one significant event which was not properly dealt with by myself and, at least in my mind, I had taken full responsibility for it. My senior colleague was imposing significant restrictions on my practice. There were heated emotional arguments in that meeting. I was quite angry with the way it was dealt with. It seemed like the whole world was against me, except for my immediate family. I was given only one option; to work in a significantly restricted environment with intense supervision at all times. I was furious and stormed out of the meeting, handing in my resignation on spot. There was just no time for reflection.

Can you imagine what happened to me next? Just 9 months into moving to a new country and I was now jobless with a family to support, and with 10 complaints hanging over me. I was extremely angry and distressed. How would I support my family? How would I deal with these challenging situations? Furthermore, I had to look for a new job in a new country.

It was 6.30pm that evening. I was not able to think properly. My wife, who has always been supportive, consoled me. But it was not helping. I had to vent my anger and frustration at the whole turn of events. It was 7 pm and drizzling outside. So, I decided to run physically. I wasn't running away from my challenges but moving towards solutions. Our home is quite high up on a mountain slope, so I ran all the way from the mountain top to the rail station. The whole series of events from the last few months played out in my mind. Although I was quite disturbed initially, things started to make a bit of sense after one hour of running.

I came back home a couple of hours later as I had been running in the rain and had to walk back up the steep mountain. The physical exhaustion was nothing compared to my inner turmoil. However, running provided me with insight and clarity. Here I was in a new country; jobless, with serious complaints holding me down. Tension was building in my head and I felt that I couldn't just stay at home and think about it all day. I explored all my options in terms of medical defense and decided to work at weekends during this time. I decided to be proactive and I called an employment agency the next day. From that call, I managed to secure a weekend job in Sydney.

A few days later, I received the dreaded letter in my inbox detailing all the complaints lodged against me. The nature of complaints was significant and meant my medical registration could be in jeopardy. It made out that I was a health professional who's main focus was only to make money and that I didn't care about my patients at all. It was by far the most challenging event of my life. It shook me to my inner core. Was I not a good doctor? Did I not look after my patients well? Was my main focus only to make money? Was I being true to myself and my profession?

I had to answer all these questions to myself first, before anyone else in the world. It was not easy to manage all on my own, with such a major chain of events. Fortunately, I was blessed with a supportive family and I got help from the medical defense, a good, helpful friend who listened and, finally, my own discipline, willpower, motivation and a keen desire to turn things around.

The 7-morning habits that I had been practicing for the previous 7-8 years became my most important friends. They helped me become the master of my own destiny. I have an absolutely firm conviction that these habits have had such a strong and positive influence, that they could help anyone overcome any adversity. Life's problems and setbacks will still come and go.

All challenges are like ocean waves which come at regular intervals, then go away, only to strike us once more. Some are small harmless waves; others are big and have the capacity to engulf us. It is entirely up to us to decide whether we wish to consider ourselves as strong rocks on the ocean shore, which stay sturdy, or tiny pebbles which are swept away by huge waves. I wish to reaffirm that that anyone can become stronger and more resilient by consistently practicing these powerful habits. Waking up early is the foremost 7-star habit. Practicing these seven habits significantly sharpens our focus and sets the tone for the day, helping us become MASTERS of our own destiny.

MASTERS is an acronym which I will discuss in-depth later, but for now, it stands for:

M - Meditate and Be Mindful
A - Action your Affirmations
S - Smile + Be Silent
T - Think + Thank
E - Exercise
R - Read
S - Share your Story + Scribble

I reflected on my options. I could have resigned and gone back to my homeland and practiced medicine there. In fact, having got a postgraduate degree from India, this would have been a very easy option. I would have made much more money and had the luxury of extended family support. I could have returned to the UK, but the complaint would still have been looming. Then, I had the obvious option of staying and fighting my case in Australia. Finally, I had the choice of not only fighting my case but seeing it as a stepping stone for future success. It did not take me long; I decided to go for the final option.

In the first 4-5 weeks when I was jobless, I had time for reflection and introspection. It felt like I had hit a wall; I was feeling depressed and playing the role of victim. Throughout my entire working life - nearly two decades - I had never been unemployed. So, it was a highly stressful and anxious period. But I was still practicing MASTERS. Slowly, positivity started filling my mind. Thoughts and ideas began to sprout. How about the idea of starting a family community practice, where we worked as self-employed professionals? Where should I start? How should I start? There were 1001 questions running through my mind. I had to start somewhere.

So, I decided to explore the whole area of Wollongong (a city just one hour drive from Sydney, Australia) all the way from the northern to the most southern suburbs. I physically visited all these areas from morning 'til night on the weekdays (when I was jobless). I also made a point of meeting and chatting to the local doctors and staff in the medical practices across the whole region. Google maps and Wikipedia lent their insights into the demographics of the whole area. Various other government websites helped me to figure out the fundamental requirements of opening a general practice. On reflection, while I was essentially jobless, my days were entirely full.

I was still working at the weekends to ensure that some money was coming in. My wife was still working at the same practice where the complaint had been made. She was working to ensure that a steady income was coming into the household. I was completely opposed to the idea of her working in a place where the complaint had been made, yet she managed really well. It was not easy for her to do this day in and day out. Perhaps I was not proactive enough to help her get a job elsewhere. I believe now, that I was so engrossed in my own issues that I had little time to think about her. There were arguments at home and as a family, it was a highly stressful time.

In about 6 weeks' time, I was finally able to secure a full-time job locally under the supervision of a very good clinician, whilst the complaint was ongoing. My supervisor was very helpful and supportive and the staff there were loving and kind. I was not seeing many patients at that time. So, I devoted my free time to my own learning. I studied a combination of online learning modules, self-help inspiring books and medical magazines. I also listened to motivational audio tapes and videos.

Due to the nature of the complaints - and the number - the higher authorities had no option but to interview me physically. I had to attend the complaint offices in Sydney. It felt like I was a criminal who had committed a serious, heinous crime (when in reality, no harm was done to any patient). I was accompanied by a member of my medical defense.

It was indeed like a magistrate's court. There were two senior medical doctors who were trained in hearing such complaints and one non-medical attendee. They checked all the documents being presented to them. I was supported by one medical doctor and one member of non-medical support personnel. There was a huge table in between the two parties, and I was the focus of the attention. The complaint file was huge; approximately 250 pages of paperwork.

The legal process then began. I was allowed to give a brief overview of my life from the very beginning as a medical student, to the point of the hearing. The cross-examination started with the first complaint. The investigating officers went into every minute detail of my consultation. They asked me questions, one after another. It was a highly taxing and stressful process. Yes, there were supporting officers from the medical defense, but I had to answer all the questions in detail.

To make matters more challenging, the complainant had sent dozens of faxes to the court in the early hours of the morning, to make the case stronger. My defense objected to this and we were given 20 minutes to go through all the new material. I had never been to a criminal court in my life but to me, it really felt like I had committed a terrible crime, and that all the evidence was being collected and sent in to prove that I was liable.

The first complaint was the most severe, and the only one which was important in terms of patient safety. I told the court instantly and honestly that I was completely responsible for the error, and that it may have had potentially significant consequences. But, in reality, no harm was done to any of my patients. Rest of the issues were meant to strengthen the complainant's case. I was asked a multitude of questions by the investigating officers and I answered honestly.

In total, I was questioned for nearly 5 hours with some mini breaks in between. It was lunchtime and I was feeling terribly mentally exhausted. My defense team were very highly supportive and helped me get a sandwich from a local cafeteria. Post-lunch, I was asked further series of questions related to the complaint and was told that the outcome of the hearing would come in an email. It was devastating. I wanted to know what they wanted from me. What now? What next? I was advised that I would get the notification in a week's time. The waiting was killing me.

In the end, an email came from the higher authorities, stating that I had to do work under the supervision of an experienced clinician. My mentor was advised to give quarterly reports of my clinical performance. I was working even more diligently and cautiously now. My supervisor was quite happy with my progress and gave good reports to the higher bodies. The whole process was slow and tedious. There were deadlines attached and implications linked with non-compliance. It was serious.

MASTERS helped me during all the trials, tribulations and challenging times. It was the key framework which helped me maintain my self-confidence, perseverance and resilience. I was also getting help and support from my immediate family, my parents who were still in India, one close friend and my external medical defense. I have always had a deep sense of gratitude for all these strong pillars of support. Both these two pillars of support, help from outside and inner toughness are equally important. However, ultimately you have to take responsible action. No matter how much love and external support you get, you will fundamentally have to face your challenges yourself. Nobody else in the world will do it for you.

The months were passing slowly. I was working full-time and as I was only seeing a few patients, I decided to also see nursing home patients to increase my income. In the early hours of morning, I would meditate, read, reflect, run and write. We also applied for consent to develop and build a practice in an old house in a nearby suburb. The application was rejected on 2 occasions over a period of twelve slow, tedious months. But we were fortunate the third time. I was able to do this work because I believed in proactivity, hard work and responsibility. We had a vision of doing real, meaningful work in our specialty - to take on challenges during tough times. Now, I always remember and follow this quote: "When the going gets tough, the tough get going."

After 9 months of supervision, I was advised that the medical investigators would come to my practice, see my consulting style and decide whether I was now okay to practice independently. They sat with me during my consultations and watched me with patients. They watched and took notes. It was a highly stressful scenario. Imagine: two investigators with me and a patient, cramped into a very small room. At the same time, one other investigator was scrutinizing my notes from the previous consultations over the previous few months, in another room. Then, it was lunchtime.

Post-lunch, they gave me six scenarios and I had to go through them, orally. To me, it felt like sitting my membership exam again. I was confident in answering their questions and felt I had done well. I was told the outcome of this investigation would come in 1-2 weeks. I was fairly optimistic that it would all end for the better. Astonishingly, an email arrived a week later, advising that though I was satisfactory in most consultations and scenarios, I still had to continue with supervision and see the final advisory committee 4 months later. I was very despondent and deeply frustrated by the outcome.

I was in regular touch with my defense team. They told me that I had two options; either to play the role of a victim, act defensively, be reactive and let the case go on for quite some time. The other option was to keep persevering. I made up my mind that day, that I would be extremely proactive. Be a responsible man. Live life as a lifelong learner. I would see these challenges and setbacks as stepping stones for success. I would practice the MASTERS consistently, every day.

I started making a journal entry a day in my black diary. Motivational, inspirational self-help books were some of my biggest friends. I would go outside for a light jog or workout on our cross-trainer. Playing squash weekly with my close friend also helped me vent my frustration. I had visualized myself, deep down, as a winner in the grand scheme of things, and that feeling would remain with me throughout the day. I was devoted to giving my best shot in front of the final advisory committee.

One day prior to the day of the big decision, I collated all my journal entries and emailed them to the advisory committee. I glanced at all the books that had helped me profoundly during challenging times and collected the most important ones. I took all the medical books and the black diary, where I had been making journal entries every day for the last 3-4 months. Finally, the day arrived. My defense team told me it was likely to be intense and the decision could be literally anything from remaining under supervision, doing more exams, to more favorable outcomes. I was mentally prepared for the best and worst outcomes - and anything in between. There was a panel of three people; two doctors and one member of non-medical personnel. When we were called, I entered the room with three bags. Two were full of books which had influenced me most and one contained all the material pertaining to the complaints. My defense team accompanied me.

I opened the bags and neatly set up all the books and preparation material in the corners of the big desk. The advisory committee went through the paperwork. They wanted my response. I had the option of being critical, negative and sarcastic. But deep in my heart, I was aware this approach was not going to be helpful. I portrayed myself as a lifelong student, a learner who was committed to helping myself and contributing to society. So, my responses were universally positive, showing my willingness to learn from anybody in all aspects of life. I was not even thinking about the complaints anymore. It was more about healing and rehabilitation.

The advisory committee interviewed me for approximately one hour. They asked me what my plans were in the future. I replied that we were keen on opening a community medical practice in the near future, with the idea of serving and contributing to society. They called a break, during which we were allowed to go outside, and I could have a chat with my defense team.

We were called back in after the break. I could immediately sense positive vibes in the investigating rooms. It was far more relaxed. The body language of the investigating officers said it all. They were open, relaxed and had smiles on their faces. When we were seated, they announced that they had been impressed with my performance, core values, discipline and the tools I had used to improve myself on a daily basis during these challenging times. I was given the all-clear by the committee and all my restrictions were lifted.

I was deeply and genuinely happy that this day had finally arrived, and my preparation and learning had ultimately bought tangible results. I thanked the jury and the investigating officers with tears in my eyes and pledged that I would continue to commit to daily learning and contribute to our community. We left the room and I thanked my defense team with a smile that was full of deep gratitude.

My defense team was happy yet surprised. According to them, it was the first time that such a trial had finished so quickly.

Apparently, it was more normal for these things to last a couple of years or more, especially in complex cases such as mine, which had only lasted a total of 15 months. Also, the trial time on the final day had been one hour, which was quite unprecedented. Soon after, I called my loving wife and delivered the good news. She was deeply happy, and I could sense her tears in the tone of her voice. I also called my parents In India, who were genuinely happy for me. Finally, I called my close friend and thanked him for helping me during the challenging times.

During all these trials and tribulations, I had also been actively researching and working on opening our practice in a friendly community. I got involved with builders, development authority personnel, an IT department and various government organizations. There were significant challenges and obstacles at each step. It was exactly 4 months since the end of the complaint that we were able to open our community medical practice. It was a moment of immense pride and joy. The following year, we became an accredited practice and started teaching medical students. Now, we mentor and train GP registrars - the future GPs of Australia. Life has come full circle and I expect more challenges to come so that we can grow further.

We have done this and have a firm belief that you can do this in your respective fields. You may feel my story's context is completely different to yours; however, the challenges and emotions will still resonate with you – of that, I am sure. It really does depend on our mindset. It relies heavily on our internal beliefs, core values and clarity of what exactly we want to do. Whenever I reflect on how we have achieved all this, I feel it is a combination of inner resilience and external support from our family, friends and other team members. MASTERS is a 7 habit framework which helped me navigate this journey with a firm determination to view myself as a winner.

Just recently, I did something unimaginable. I met the vehicle of my challenges (face to face), yes the complainant after full 4 yrs. The meeting went well and we had a conversation for some time and I genuinely thanked him for being the vehicle of my challenges. My family and friends thought- I was crazy. Either of us may have become defensive or there may be heated arguments. None of that happened and it was a good closure to this story. This is what I wrote in my letter which I personally handed to him.

Hello, Dr. (Name excluded),

I hope you are very well and in good health. I understand that all events happened in the past for a reason. Today, I have come to express my sincere gratitude.

I honestly hated you when it all started, but not anymore.

I have realized you were the vehicle of my challenges. I have grown and prospered all because of you. We never had a plan to open our own practice, when we moved to Australia. The challenges I encountered during all the trials and tribulations made me resilient. Had you not been there, I may not have encountered challenges and perhaps would not have grown. I firmly believe that all growth happens due to significant challenges in our lives. I sincerely take this opportunity to express my genuine thank you. This is to let you know that I have moved on. At the same time, I wish to tell you that I do not have any bad feelings against you. Moreover, I wish that you grow, prosper and bring light in the lives of people we serve.

Thanks very much

Your colleague
Dr. Priank Gupta

The purpose of sharing my hitherto untold story is to let you harness the seeds of a proactive attitude, a winner's mindset and a responsible behavior. It is absolutely not to glorify myself; rather, it is to empower you, my dear readers. I am not after any fame or material wealth for myself in the grand scheme of things. I will consider myself successful if you take ideas from this or any other stories and, most importantly, apply them to your life.

You must have a firm conviction that you can turn things around. You must transform the stumbling blocks into stepping stones of success.
Say to yourself, "I have all the confidence that I need now.
I love myself. I am the number one supporter of myself."
We should internalize (feel) and visualize (see) these strong positive emotions and thoughts, as they are highly powerful and make us stronger every day.
But most importantly, we should action them.

Science and Art of happiness

We all want to be happy. It is a fact. A quick search on Amazon brings up more than two hundred thousand books on happiness. Clearly, everyone on the planet wishes to be happier than ever! Happiness is a mental or emotional state of well-being defined by positive or pleasant emotions ranging from contentment to intense joy. Research shows that happiness is not the result of bouncing from one material item to the next. Achieving and maintaining happiness involves periods of considerable discomfort, challenges, and facing and overcoming struggles in a meaningful way.

Money is still important to happiness, but only to a certain degree. Money buys freedom from worry about the basics in life — food, clothing and housing. Aspects such as genetic makeup, life circumstances, achievements, marital status, social relationships - even our neighbors - all influence how happy we can be. A family earning a combined income of $6250/month, equating to $75,000 per year, is the magic number in the western world. The equivalent figure may, of course, be relatively low in the developing world. Below this figure, our happiness levels do increase with increasing salary, however, they plateau after this threshold. This is such an important fact, which has been gathered after significant scientific research.

Our happiness levels do not increase if we keep on accumulating material wealth after reaching a tally of $75000 annually. Sure, it will allow us to buy more shiny things, but the happiness linked with these material objects will only be temporary. Research and experience have proven this time and again. At this point, I would like you to stop reading the book for a few moments. Close your eyes. Reflect on this important fact.

Happiness Quotient

In 2000, Dr. Martin Seligman and his colleagues started studying the positive elements of human life, like positive emotions and happiness. They created a new branch of research named Positive Psychology. In 2002, Dr. Seligman published a book on happiness - Authentic Happiness. The book encapsulates years of research into practical and simple guidelines for living a happier life. At the very core of the book lies his formula for happiness. It is a simple yet powerful tool of all the elements that impact our happiness.

The Happiness Formula

H = S + C + V

100 %= 50 %+ 10 % + 40 %

- *H* - Our enduring level of *happiness* = 100%
- *S* - our *set* range = 50%
- *C* - the *circumstances* in our life = 10%
- *V* - represents factors under our *voluntary* control= 40%

H: Our Enduring level of happiness-100%

It's important to differentiate between our momentary levels of happiness (simple pleasures) and our enduring levels of happiness (also called our blissful state or pure joy). Momentary happiness is increased by little pleasures like basking in warm sunshine during cold winters, sipping a freshly brewed coffee, listening to birds singing, watching the sunrise or sunset and a myriad of other day to day beautiful moments. They are important in our living a mindful life, actively paying attention to simple daily pleasures and relishing our experiences!

Enduring happiness is a much deeper and sustained emotion. It gives us a degree of rare satisfaction which lasts for much longer; even after the end of an experience. Examples of this include volunteering, contributing to a charity, or working in the community. The whole message is that we are actively helping our fellow humans, our planet or other endangered species. Importantly, the amount doesn't matter. What truly matters is the underlying spirit of an altruistic activity, as it lies at the heart of such beautiful acts of kindness. These most definitely bring about an ecstatic state of lasting happiness.

S: Our Set range - 50 %

About 50 percent of our happiness is not under our control as it depends on our genetic makeup. We may be genetically wired to be quite happy or sad most of the time, or it may be somewhere in the middle. Our genes account for 50 percent of our happiness, and that can't be changed. We have a sort of happiness set point to which we will always gravitate - in good times as well as bad. Buying a new car, getting your work published, going on holidays, meeting your future spouse - each may raise your happiness levels for a while but, in a few months or years, it will shift back to your set point. This happens because of adaptation.

Human beings are adaptive machines. We take good things for granted and overcome significant challenges only to return back to our natural happiness set points. For example, lottery winners are happier for a few months but soon revert to their baseline. Some of them resign from their jobs, thinking that they don't need to work. But they can't find any purpose for their huge amounts of money and return back to their jobs after some time. People fired from their jobs will be stressed for a few weeks or months, but then gravitate to their setpoints. They find other avenues for their happiness. Even individuals who become paraplegic (lose their legs strength and mobility) as a result of spinal cord injuries, quickly adapt to their greatly limited capacities and, within 6-8 weeks, report more net positive emotions than negative feelings. Within a few years, they are only slightly less happy on an average than humans who are not paralyzed.

We all have a set range of happiness towards which we naturally gravitate. Miraculously though, we can use other parameters; C and V - to boost this level.

C: Circumstances - 10%

If we wish to augment our levels of happiness by changing the external circumstances of our lives, these strategies may help.

- Living in a wealthy democratic country (a strong effect)
- Getting married (a robust effect)
- Avoiding negative events and emotions (moderate effect)
- Involvement in rich social connections (a dynamic potent effect)
- Finding religion (a moderate effect)

Changing these circumstances is either impractical, expensive or practically impossible for many. And even if we can alter one or all of the above, it won't make much of a difference anyway. Why? Because they account for roughly 10% of total happiness levels. The good news is that there are a set of internal circumstances that are relatively easy to change and will have a far greater impact on our happiness.

V: Voluntary variables - 40%

If we really want to change our enduring levels of happiness, we have to focus on these important voluntary factors, as they are under our control. They account for 40 percent of our happiness levels and are subdivided into three types:

- Positive emotions about the past (e.g. satisfaction, contentment, fulfillment, pride, serenity, peace)
- Positive emotions about the future (e.g. optimism, hope, faith, belonging, trust, being vulnerable and accepting the unknown)
- Positive emotions about the present (e.g. joy, calm, challenges viewed from a positive frame of mind, enthusiasm, pleasure, and flow)

The more positive emotions we have about the past, future, and present, the happier we will be. Hence, to augment our enduring levels of happiness, we have to fundamentally modify the way we feel about our past, how we think about the future, and how we relish our present. This book explores how we can change these voluntary factors which are under our direct control. The MASTERS framework comprises the habits we apply intentionally to modify them.

Story of Big Rocks, Pebbles, Sand and Water

A university professor walks into a chemistry class and sets a big glass jar on the table. He silently places several 5-6 cm sized rocks into the jar until no more can fit inside. He asks the class if the jar is full and all the students agree it is.

He says, "Really?" and pulls out a pile of small pebbles - about half the size of the big rocks- and adds them to the jar, shaking it gently until they fill the spaces in between the big rocks. He asks again, "Is the jar full?" The students again agree.

Next, he adds a scoop of sand to the jar, filling the space between the pebbles and asks the same question yet again. This time, the class is hesitant, some feeling that the jar is obviously full, but others were thinking that there is yet another trick coming. Anyway, he grabs a flask of water and fills the jar to the brim, saying, "If this jar is your life, what does this experiment mean?" A bold student replies, "No matter how busy we think we are; we can always take on more." "That is one view," the professor replies.

Then he make eye contact with all the students. "The big rocks represent the big things in our lives – what we will value at the end of our life – our families, our spouses, our health, accomplishing our aspirations and dreams, and leaving a legacy. The pebbles are the other things in our lives that give it meaning, like our jobs, our homes, our hobbies and our friendships. The sand and water represent the 'small stuff' that fills our time, like watching TV or mindlessly spending time on social media.

Looking out at the class again, he asks, "Can we see what would happen if we started with the sand or the pebbles?" Would we be able to fit the same number of big rocks inside - those which are truly important and matter the most?"

This story is a masterpiece, underpinning the timeless principle of making a habit of keeping our most important rocks as our highest priorities. Every life is valuable, and we should all actively reflect and examine:

- What are the big rocks in our lives?
- What are the small rocks or pebbles in our lives?
- What activities represent sand in our lives?

I encourage you to write the answers in your journal, or even here. The best time to write is early in the morning, when the rest of your family is asleep, or at any other time when you can't be disturbed. The simple act of writing answers is the first step towards knowing yourself. This is a highly rewarding activity and miraculously, subconsciously, you will gravitate towards spending more time on your big rocks. This is a big win for you

My life's big rocks, small rocks and sand...

My Big Rocks in Life
My Small rocks of life
Sand of my life

What do we stand for? What is your Story?

A clear vision helps individuals and companies to succeed and prosper. A story simplifies our core values. It is how we project ourselves to society. When we started the project of opening our own practice, we asked few important questions (I am using we - as the practice was opened with full help and support of my loving wife Priyanka, who is also a GP).

1. What is our aim?
2. Why are we doing it?
3. What are our guiding principles?
4. What are our core values?

We wanted to make a difference in the lives of a community we served. Our main job was to look after sick people in our community. We wanted to make a long-lasting impact; not a short-term gain, but a long-term relationship with the clients we serve. Hence, building a medical center wouldn't have worked for our story. Yes, that would have helped us make a lot of money faster. But it wouldn't have given us the degree of satisfaction we crave by looking after our clients well. The extent of the happiness we get by seeing our clients getting better week by week, and sometimes over months, is a very beautiful feeling which can't exactly be described in words. It most certainly can't and shouldn't be measured in monetary terms. Sometimes, we are moved to tears when we see their conditions improve so well.

With this in mind, we decided to open up a community general practice and name it- Horsley Community Doctors. We are centrally located and look after kids, young parents, their families, seniors, pregnant mums and people with different levels of physical and mental ability. We cater to rich and poor alike - in a nutshell, everyone in our small community. We thought a lot and decided to keep the guiding principles short and simple. We described them in 3 words: Positive, Polite, Professional. We abide by them day in, day out. They are printed on our letterheads and engraved on our name badges, which are close to our hearts.

We also spent time crafting our mission statement or guiding force. This is it:

"Our mission is to help individuals and societies reach their peak potential by adopting healthy lifestyle choices, and a state of flow and balance in their lives. We believe in providing holistic compassionate care to our community. The abundance and wellbeing achieved will help the excellent physical, mental, spiritual and family health of all community members."

The power of a story conveys its message, culture, and uniqueness to clients all around the globe. What is your unique story? Your truth and special qualities you bring to enrich our planet? We should all deeply reflect on our own stories.

I encourage all readers to write their own stories in one-page format. They should ideally be centered around the 4 questions mentioned above. Once we have a clear why, the what and how of our story will start emerging relatively easily.

My own Story

1. What is my aim?

2. Why am I doing it?

3. What are my guiding principles?

4. What are my core values?

Story of Importance versus Urgency

I consider myself a decent family man. I live with my loving wife and beautiful kids. Approximately 8 years ago while I was practising In the UK, I was working full time and more. I would do weekends and sometimes night shifts. My wife and kids would ask for family time and I would say "Love, I am doing all this for you and the kids for their future." My family just gave up on me. I was adamant and immature.

One fine weekend morning, I had to attend an important meeting out of the town. However, this meeting was scheduled just hours after the finish of my night shift. I was exhausted after the busy night shift. Initially, I thought of not going to the meeting, but it was important. My wife also advised me not to drive for safety reasons. However, I ignored all of her good intentions. As I drove past my hometown onto the freeway, I fell asleep at the wheel. My car skidded and I was lucky to narrowly miss a big passing truck. It was a real near-miss. I pulled my car over to a safe place and slept nonstop for few hours. I had been fortunate to avoid what could have been a tragic accident of my life. Later that day I reflected on this incident and decided not to do any more night shifts and to significantly cut down the weekend work as well.

I decided to spend more time with my family and live in the Now, not the future.

This story demonstrates the important concepts of importance and urgency. An esteemed author and leadership consultant, the late Mr. Stephen Covey beautifully illustrated this in his book, "The 7 habits of highly effective people." We have to decide what the most important things in our lives are. On our deathbed, what memories we will cherish? Time spent with our loved ones, a dream or a mission which impacts society and contributes to the community? Or material possessions and power over others during our lifetimes? These are important questions and require careful reflection, introspection and a deep study of the self.

We need to categorize our activities on the basis of importance and urgency.

1. Highly urgent and important.
2. Highly important, non-urgent.
3. Urgent to others, not important to us.
4. Non-urgent, not important.

Quad 1	Quad 2
HIGHLY URGENT AND IMPORTANT Examples 1. Official and other deadlines. 2. Medical emergencies. 3. Pressing issues. 4. Last minute problems. 5. Unexpected events. 6. Natural disasters. **Solution** - Action it ASAP!	**HIGHLY IMPORTANT, NON-URGENT** Examples 1. Written goals. 2. Planning. 3. True connections. 4. Relationships with family and friends. 5. Team building. 6. Character development. 7. Cultivating a winning mindset. 8. Time spent with family. 9. Contributing to the community. 10. Leaving a legacy. **Solution** - Planning short, medium and long-term goals
Quad 3	**Quad 4**
URGENT TO OTHERS, NOT IMPORTANT TO US Examples 1. Most Email notifications. 2. Some phone calls. 3. Satisfying other people's priorities and expectations. 4. Saying yes when you actually want to say No. 5. Being busy in work all the time. **Solution** - Cut down or Delegate	**NON-URGENT, NOT IMPORTANT** Examples 1. Addiction to social media. 2. Mindless watching of the TV. 3. Surfing the Internet just for the sake of killing time. 4. Watching negative news. 5. Some Emails. 6. Some phone calls and texts. 7. Senseless gossip. 8. Meeting and spending time with negative people. **Solution** - Cut it out / Avoid it as much as you can!

Practical Action Strategies

We must realize how much time are we spending on all these respective quadrants. The quality of our lives will ultimately depend on the time we spend on Quadrant 2, because it is where we actually grow.

Quadrant 1 is forced on us if we do not devote enough time to Quadrant 2; for example, all the quality relationships within a family or teamwork in the office, take considerable time and effort. It is simple to understand, yet not easy to implement day after day and year after year. It requires perseverance and immense dedication to our true selves. Just imagine, if you do not spend a good quantity and quality time with your family, what will happen? Yes, you are right. The relationships will suffer and likely lead to mental health problems, which will bring us to Quadrant 1 (the quadrant in which we don't want to be, at least intentionally)

Quadrant 3 is all about deleting and delegating these tasks. It takes effort to identify which tasks are in quadrant 3 and then delegating them to the right person.

Quadrant 4 is mostly crap. We don't want to invest our valuable time here.

Just to get an approximate idea, these are the times spent in these quadrants by people:

Quadrant 1	Quadrant 2
Ordinary and Reactive - 30%	Ordinary and Reactive - 10%
Smart and Efficient - 20%	Smart and Efficient - 20%
Wise leader - 10%	Wise leader - 80%
Quadrant 3	**Quadrant 4**
Ordinary and Reactive - 30%	Ordinary and Reactive - 30%
Smart and Efficient - 40%	Smart and Efficient - 20%
Wise leader - 10%	Wise leader - 0%

You can decide in which category you belong currently, but our priority should be to spend most of our time in Quadrant 2, as it is the one in which we find genuine happiness and true joy.

Story of Gratefulness

A blind boy was sitting on the steps of a skyscraper with a hat by his feet. He was holding up a sign which said, 'I am blind, please help.' There were only a couple of coins in his hat. A man was walking by. He took a few coins from his pocket and dropped them into the hat. He then took the sign, turned it around, and wrote some words. He reversed the sign so that every passerby would see the new words. Soon the hat began to fill up. A lot more people were giving money to the blind boy. That evening, the man who had changed the sign came back to see how things were. The boy instantly recognized his footsteps and asked, "Are you the one who changed my sign this morning? What did you write? " The man said, "I only wrote the truth. I said what you said but in a different way." I wrote - "Today is a beautiful day, but I cannot see it."

Both signs told people that the boy was blind. But the first sign simply said that the boy was blind. The second sign showed people that they were so lucky because they weren't. It helped them become more grateful and compassionate. Bearing this in mind, does it come as a surprise that the second sign was so highly effective?

Be eternally grateful for what we have. Be innovative. Think uniquely, differently and positively. We all have unique talents and tapping into these powers requires a measure of gratitude.

Countless studies have proven that the practice of gratitude is immensely powerful and makes a person genuinely happy. Not cosmetically, but really deep within. The beauty of this approach is that a grateful person is happy, and they subconsciously make others happy. Their positive vibes rub off on others they meet. This, in turn, makes them even happier. So, it is a never-ending positive, harmonious cycle.

Action steps

1. Make a daily list of 5 things you are grateful for – this could be your spouse, kids, or other family members. You could also include things like being alive today. Getting your daily bread and water. Having a good sleep. Enjoying a beautiful sunrise or sunset. Being grateful for your work because it gives you purpose. Being grateful for freshly made coffee by a barista. Being grateful to the pizza delivery boy/ girl. The list is endless. Just start...
2. When to do it – Ideally, first thing in the morning as the positive effects of this sacred practice bring profound happy effects immediately, which then last throughout the day. However, it can be done anytime, anywhere. The effects are always positive and incremental.
3. Consistency is the key. It takes 1-2 minutes to do this practice. There is simply no excuse for not having the time to do it. So, we must do it daily.
4. How to do it - Get a small journal or a diary, along with a colored pencil or pen. Colors are magical. Write the date. Start writing! A short prayer will also do the same.
5. Measure your happiness levels on a scale of 1-10 at the beginning and end of 6-8 weeks of this sacred experiment. You will be surprised how much your happiness levels have increased at the end of the experiment.

Story of Empowering Girls

Oliver is a skateboard teacher working for Skateistan, a nonprofit organization that combines skateboarding and education as a tool for empowering young people. Half the population of Afghanistan is currently under the age of 16, and 70% of the population is under 25. It is quite shocking what role women play in society; most of them don't have jobs and are not allowed to go to school. It's even been deemed culturally inappropriate for them to ride bikes! Skateboarding, however, is so popular in Afghanistan that nobody has had a chance to forbid girls from doing it. So, they skate!

Oliver earns $10 a week, and he has electricity every couple of days, yet he is constantly rewarded by his time with the kids - showing them how to skate, teaching them valuable skills in the classroom and taking them on field trips around Kabul. He was even able to help a 12-year-old girl, Priscilla, get a job as a skateboarding instructor, so she could stop begging on the streets and work to support her entire family.

But Skateistan is not without its heartbreak. In April 2015, four of the school's students were killed in a suicide bombing at the NATO facility in Kabul. The community rallied together to help the families of the children who passed away, and at the skatepark, a boy skated up and down the ramps in honor of his deceased brother. Today, in Afghanistan, 40% of skateboarders are girls. Skateboarding is now the largest female sport in the country, and Skateistan continues to use it to educate and empower girls and boys in the community.

This real-life story constantly reminds us of the important tasks that need to be done. Helping the underprivileged and most disadvantaged humans on the planet is a worthy goal. It brings us deep enduring satisfaction and happiness. In this story, Oliver earns a measly sum, not even being able to access the most basic amenities of daily life. Yet, he stays there. He is living life in a danger zone. The threat to his life is always there, yet he persists and perseveres. The overarching mission to improve the life of these young kids is such a worthy cause that he doesn't care about his own survival. I believe we can all learn from Oliver.

All research suggests that there is significant gender inequality globally. In the third world and developing countries, millions of girls are subjected to abuse, child labor, trafficking, child marriage and other offenses. Girls in poor communities often miss school because of a lack of clean water in their villages. Instead of attending class, girls and women globally spend countless hours fetching water that is often dirty and dangerous for their health. Many thousands of women still die annually due to complications during pregnancy or childbirth and thousands of children die every day, mostly from preventable and treatable causes such as pneumonia, diarrhea, and malaria.

In the developed world, there are significant issues of pay inequality, harassment and bullying in the workplace, sexual abuse… the list goes on.

Action steps you can implement

There are simple ways to support women locally and globally.

1. Appreciate women in your life - wife, sister, daughter and staff at work force for the kind help, they provide day in day out.
2. Make a charitable donation to the organization you believe eg- The global women's project, International women's development agency overseas aid fund, Domestic violence crisis service, World vision.
3. Invest in female business owners.
4. Directly thank women for their kind gestures, much of which frequently goes unpaid and unnoticed. Acknowledge their efforts toward helping the team, the family, or the household. Express your gratitude for even small actions they have taken, such as refilling the copier paper, turning a report in early, making and serving food on our dinner table everyday.
5. Ensure that we don't just complement only their beauty, but also other aspects of their personality like being brilliant, brave, kind and dedicated.

Story of Marathon of Hope

I did a tandem skydive many years ago. At that time, I was working in the UK alongside an esteemed professor of general practice. I was very happy and excited. When I expressed my feelings to the professor, she remarked, "Good on you". I was a bit disheartened, as I was expecting more praise. Later, I reflected and asked myself, "Good on you? What does this mean exactly? Only good for me. Not good for anyone else. No contribution here. No meaningful cause. Anyway, I continued my work with her in general practice.

A couple of months later, I found myself encouraging my young teenage daughter to do some fast cycling, as she was not gaining height through an early teenage growth spurt. To motivate her, I said, "You bike on the cycle path and I will run behind you". She started cycling and I started running. It was early hours of morning. I discovered that running is so good for our minds, bodies and souls. Soon, the 500 metres turned into 1 km, 2 km and so on. I started enjoying the process. Eventually, my daughter lost interest in cycling, but I continued running. Once I hit the 5 km mark, I told myself that I would do a full marathon. And this time not for me, but for an important cause. I planned to complete a full marathon in 6 months and raise money for a local hospice. I visualised myself doing all the groundwork, practice and bought all the equipment I needed.

I planned to do a half marathon in 3 months and build stamina after that. Events happened as I planned. To ensure I was successful, I did a full practice marathon 1 week prior to the actual event. We raised $1500 for this event.

Finally, the day arrived. There were hundreds of marathon runners. Some were running for personal goals and achievements. Some of them were blind and running with their assistants. Some were dressed as clowns and running to raise important funds. I was amazed to learn that millions of pounds were raised in the event for various causes. I was happy that I was also part of something meaningful. I finished the marathon with a genuine smile and happiness. Next day, I told my professor about the event. She replied compassionately, "Really good, Priank. I am very happy. You have made a difference." Finally, I understood the contrast between personal gains and meaningful community contributions.

The purpose of this story is certainly not to glorify myself. Far from it. It is to empower you with a mindset that we are all hidden gems. We need to cultivate a growth outlook and a winner's mindset. MASTERS habits help us in achieving this and I strongly encourage you to practise them. I am deeply inspired by the story of a true champion - Terry Fox. The next story is dedicated to him.

Terry Fox is known for his Marathon of Hope – a 6,500-kilometre run across his native Canada, which he began aged just 22. The motivation? To raise awareness of cancer while raising money for cancer research, at a rate of $1 per Canadian citizen.

But Fox's inspirational story is more than one of fundraisings; four years previously, aged just 18, he had been diagnosed with bone cancer and his right leg had been amputated above the knee. In hospital, he met and made connections with many fellow cancer patients, and this solidarity, along with their incredible stories, made an activist out of him.

It was the night before his operation that he read an article about an amputee whose name was Dick Traum, running in the New York marathon. The challenges inspired him to do something extraordinary – in his own words, "I'm a dreamer. I like challenges. I don't give up. When I decided to do it, I knew I was going to go all out. There was no in-between."

The story of the Marathon of Hope is incredible in itself, yet heartbreaking at the same time. Fox started out with two friends on a relatively anonymous trip, but by the time he reached the center of Canada, he had become an icon, meeting fellow athletes, politicians and celebrities on his journey. Unfortunately, though, his journey was to come to an end after 143 days and 5,373 kilometers. His cancer had returned, his condition deteriorated, and he was forced to stop. He died on his 23rd birthday.

Fox's feats lived on, though. He raised $1.7 million prior to his death, and this rose to $10.5 million after a Canadian TV network got involved, arranging a telethon. By the next year, the amount stood at well over $20 million. Fox had inspired a generation of people, and his legacy lives on in the annual Terry Fox Run, which takes place in a staggering 60 countries and has raised over $600 million since it started in 1981.

Fox received the Companion of the Order of Canada as well as the country's sportsman of the year award, shortly before his death. But perhaps his greatest achievement was the effect he had on attitudes towards disabilities within society. Fox used his amputation as a springboard to live a fuller, more positive life,

and in doing so, he inspired countless people to take a different view of people with perceived disabilities.

This is such an inspirational story. I am deeply influenced and touched by it. We should all learn from such great champions of life. The main point of my story was to show that even an average human can achieve their goals if they are truly focussed and committed. This applies to any important goal in your life, meaningful to you and society, not just running. The idea of incorporating Terry Fox's story is mainly to get motivated by true heroes of the society.

Story of Purpose of life

"There is more fruit in a rich man's shampoo than a poor man's plate. "This sad quote illustrates the state of hunger in India and even in the developed world. While millions of people worldwide don't get the food they need to live a healthy life, the World Food Program says that "Over 66 million primary school-age children attend classes hungry across the developing world, with 23 million in Africa alone."

"Dadi Ki Rasoi," meaning "Grandma's kitchen," is a beautiful initiative started by social activist Anoop Khanna, alongside like-minded friends, almost 3 years ago. The main idea behind the project was to help provide home-cooked food to all sections of society who came their way, at a very minimal rate of 5 Indian rupees per plate; the equivalent to 10 cents per plate.

Dadi Ki Rasoi has two food stalls set up in Noida, near Delhi. Every day in the mid-morning, people from all walks of life come to the stalls to satisfy their hunger. Students, the working class, office workers, rickshaw drivers, shop owners, and passersby alike, form a queue to have lunch. Anoop and family spent a significant amount on setting up the kitchen, but today, the famous Rasoi is getting donations and support from many organizations. He spends an average of Rs 2500 (roughly 50 Dollars) a day on the ingredients and raw materials for the stall. Shopkeepers, knowing his purpose, now give him raw materials at discounted rates. Many residents contribute special meals on occasions like birthdays and wedding anniversaries. His team's wish is to provide quality food with a homely feel.

He could have attempted to provide the food for free, considering the help he gets from others who support his cause. But the main reason for the price is that it gives dignity to the person who is buying lunch. The quality of food is good as he personally supervises the preparation. Moreover, since the cost is low, anyone can enjoy a meal without worrying about money.

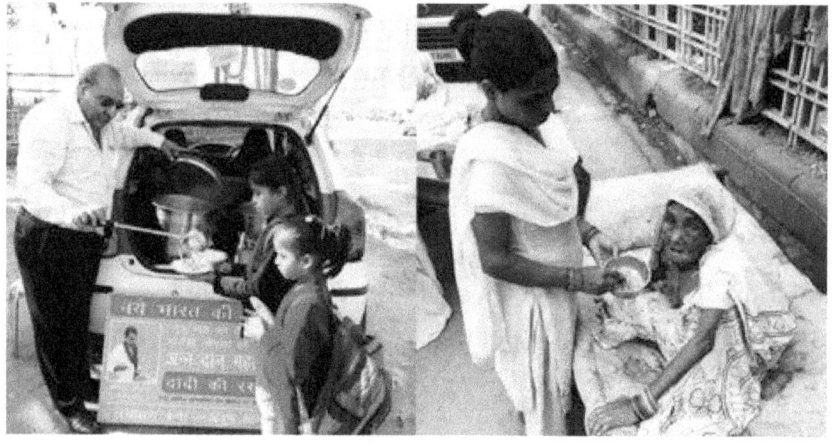

This story is touching as it is not focused on the self but on contribution. It may not be a huge contribution, but in the grand scheme of things, small, simple acts matter significantly. They make a lasting impact on our society and make it a beautiful place. The purpose of carrying out such kind acts is far from financial gain, but truly providing comfort to people who need it most. The happiness one gets through these selfless acts is meaningful and sustained.

How can *you* do these kind acts in your daily life? There are many simple ways; some of them don't even cost a penny.

Practical action steps you can implement

1. Smile at a stranger.
2. Let someone go in front of you in a queue.
3. Give a stranger a compliment.
4. Donate your old clothes to a charity or a needy person.
5. Help a senior with their groceries.
6. Prepare a meal for your family.
7. Plant a tree.
8. Do a favor without asking for anything in return.
9. Hold the elevator door for someone.
10. Write a kind or encouraging message on a napkin.
11. Pay for someone's coffee.

Story of kindness and respect

A middle-aged man boarded an airplane, arrived at his seat and saw that the passenger next to him was a poor man with an offensive smell. Quite agitated, he called the air hostess. "What's the problem, Sir?" the hostess asked. "Can't you see?" the man replied. "I have been given a seat next to this chap and he smells awful. I can't sit here next to him. You have to change my seat!" "Please, calm down, Sir," said the hostess. "Unfortunately, all the seats are occupied, but I'm still going to check if we have any." The hostess left and returned a few minutes later.

"Sir, as I told you, there are no empty seats in economy class. I spoke to the captain and he also confirmed this, but we only have one extra seat in business class." But before the man could say anything, she continued, "Sir, it is unusual for our company to allow a passenger from economy class to change to business class. However, given the circumstances, the captain thinks that it would be unfair for you to sit next to a poor person." And then, turning her gaze to the poor man, she remarked, "Which means, Sir, if you would be so kind as to pack your bag, we have reserved you a seat in business class." And all the passengers nearby, who were drawn to the scene, started cheering and gave her a standing ovation.

This story underpins the timeless principle of respect for any fellow human, regardless of class, color, caste, religion or gender. The message is priceless and signifies a deep appreciation of the core human values of equality and dignity for all fellow humans.

Practical action steps you can execute

1. Simple acts of kindness during our daily lives - smiling or saying "hello" to someone, even a stranger - are likely to boost their happiness; and even if they don't respond, our happiness levels still improve.
2. Greet your staff and clients by their first names. Greet them with a smile and a genuine, polite tone of voice.
3. Show the same degree of respect to a janitor in your company as you would a team member or a client.
4. Treat all your clients with the same respect and trust, irrespective of their financial background or the money in their pockets.
5. Book just one journey in economy class if you usually tend to travel in business class. Contribute the difference between the fares to an important cause which appeals to you. Check your own happiness levels on a scale between 1-10 (1 being the lowest and 10 being the highest - sometimes you can also score 11 or even 20 - in metaphorical terms) before the journey, then after you have made the donation.

Story of quality and quantity time

A man got a promotion in his company, so he decided to give himself a treat. He planned to go to a nearby 5-star hotel to have a meal by himself, as he could not afford the company of his friends in such an expensive restaurant.

He looked at the menu and all the prices were lavishly high. He thought, "Well, it is a 5-star hotel, so it's okay to have such extravagant prices."

So, he ordered a dessert and though the price tag was still high, he thought he could afford it. He told himself, "I am having a good time today."

The waitress came back after some time with a large, beautiful bone-china bowl. He was happy in the anticipation of a delicious dessert. But when he finally saw the portion size of the pudding, he was disheartened. He asked the waitress, "Madam, I have paid so much for this dessert and it is such a small serving!" to which she replied, "Sir, you are having a quality dessert in a 5-star restaurant. You can order more if you wish."

"But I have already paid so much. My whole wallet is empty."

"Sir, I can't help. This is how it works here."

This is an inspiring story which underpins the principles of quality versus quantity time. If we deeply reflect, both the portion size and the quality of the pudding are important. When we ask ourselves, "Is the quality time spent with the family more important than quantity of time?" the answer is both. They don't compensate for each other and ideally, there should be room for both.

Practical action steps you can execute

1. If you need more time with your spouse and your kids, make the obvious choice. Instead of watching TV or browsing social media, carve time for a family chat. Put a big-No technology zone- sign in your family room.
2. Play board games. Take a walk to a local park or sit and chat.
3. It's also vital to avoid the temptation to get kids involved in numerous activities outside the home. Some parents feel a societal pressure to sign their kids up for numerous sports teams, music and dance lessons and social clubs. This mindset does not serve anyone well. Simple family time together at mealtimes and listening to their stories, work wonders.
4. Kids don't need a dozen different weekly activities. They need *quality and quantity* time. Both are important, with loving, engaged and committed parents.

Story of staying Cocooned in our Comfort Zones

One day, a little girl was playing outdoors when she found a fascinating caterpillar. She carefully picked it up and took it home to show to her mother. Her mum allowed her to keep it, only if she looked after it well. The little girl got a large pot from her mum and put plants inside for the caterpillar to eat, and a stick to climb on. Every day, she watched the caterpillar and brought it new herbs to eat. One day, the caterpillar climbed up the stick and started acting strangely. The curious girl called her mum, who told her that the caterpillar was creating a cocoon. She explained how the caterpillar was going through a change to become a butterfly.

She was excited to hear about the changes the caterpillar would go through. She keenly watched every day, waiting for the butterfly to form. One day, a small hole appeared in the cocoon and the butterfly started to come out. At first, the girl was thrilled, but she soon became worried. The butterfly was struggling hard to come out! It looked as if it wouldn't make it. It appeared desperate! It seemed as if it was not making any progress.

The girl was so concerned she decided to help. She ran to get scissors, walked back, gently snipped the cocoon to make the hole bigger and the butterfly quickly emerged! As the butterfly came out, the girl was amazed. It had a swollen body and small, shrunken wings. She continued to watch the butterfly, hoping that now the wings would enlarge, and it would flap its wings and fly.

Sadly, none of this happened! The butterfly spent the rest of its life crawling around with a weak body and shriveled wings. It was never able to fly! The girl did not realize that her attempt to help the butterfly, had actually harmed it. The struggle to break free from the cocoon is nature's way of preparing the butterfly to learn to fly. As it fights to emerge from the restrictive cocoon, fluids from its body get pushed into the wings, making them stronger and larger, enabling them to fly. Without this struggle, the butterfly stays weak and unable to fly.

No struggles. No personal growth. No success. This is a story that is highly relevant to our lives. Most of us tend to keep ourselves in the cocoon of our "comfort zones". Our personal best only comes when we take on challenges head-on and keep working on our personal growth. These struggles make us resilient and the lessons we learn make us grow and prosper. There is no competition between ourselves and anyone else on the planet. There is only one valid competition; the only true benchmark of comparison, and that's against our past selves.

Practical action steps you can execute

1. Embark on bolder projects. It doesn't mean that you don't need to plan. You still have to take calculated risks. What it does mean though, is that you are not hesitant; make bold decisions because they take you to unchartered territory.

2. Be ready and prepared to step out of your "convenience compass." We are all relaxed and most comfortable in this zone. But true meaningful growth happens to us only when we step outside of this territory, into the realm of unknown. Yes, there are inherent risks, but the rewards are great too.
3. Instances of brave projects can be anything you love or are passionate about; for example, learning a new sport, hobby or language. Then, there are purposes that you care about; for example, volunteering and contribution.

Story of a Champion Mindset

The history of world sports is marvelous when we listen to the feats of icons like Sachin Tendulkar, Michael Phelps, Sergey Bubka, Roger Federer, Serena Williams and many other great champions. The entire world admires their talent and craft, but how about other hidden champions of our society?

Swapna Augustine, 41, didn't complain about her physical condition until she was 12. Born without both arms in a small village in Kerala, India, she believed that her arms were yet to grow out of her body. At 12, she realized the cold, bitter truth that nothing could be done about her condition and she has not looked back since! She is now an internationally acclaimed painter.

She was assisted by her mum with all activities until age 4. At 4, she was given home tuition on how to write, holding a pencil between her toes. It was not easy. Her legs didn't bend properly, and her toes hurt. But she persisted and her parents had full faith in her. Within 2 years, she had developed more flexibility in her legs and feet and was able to perform *all the activities* that anyone else could with their arms and hands. At 6, she was sent to a boarding school for children with disabilities. She met numerous other kids there with similar or worse conditions and learned how to make the best out of her perceived disability. "We were made to help each other with eating, bed transfers and other daily activities. I'm grateful to Sister Marielle and Sister Rose of Mercy Home, for what I am today. They taught me the lessons of self-reliance and independence," Swapna says.

Despite rare holiday visits thrice a year, she never stayed at home until she graduated in history from St. Mary's College, Ernakulam. During that time, she displayed her skills in drawing and painting, most of her work portraying beautiful flowers, birds and shades of nature. After attending a workshop on acrylic painting, she took up professional painting on canvas. One neighbor suggested, she join the Swiss society of art. After her application, her condition was verified, and she became a member of the International Mouth and Foot Painting Artist Association (IMFPA) in 1999. She also had to undergo rigorous training under an art teacher for nearly four years, during which she mastered both art theory and practice.

Swapna sells her paintings at IMFPA nowadays. She tells us that people born with disabilities *do not expect sympathy* from mainstream society; rather, they request public places and infrastructure which are accessible to them. She is undoubtedly the real champion in our distracted world.

She says, "There is no point feeling sad or depressed about what you do not have. God must have had a plan when he made me like this. Importantly, he gave me the gift of art." She is often asked how she is able to always smile. "Everyone, be they relatives or friends, wants us to be happy, don't you think?" she asks, and shares her thoughts about the current generation of poorly motivated students who even contemplate suicide when they don't get good grades. "They need to develop the mental strength to negotiate tough situations," she maintains.

Cultivate a Champion Mindset

1. Champions believe in themselves. They have strong voices in their minds, saying, "No matter what - I am the winner." They abide by this philosophy. Muhammad Ali famous saying, "I am the greatest," was dismissed as delusion until the whole world started believing him.
2. They put in rigorous effort daily. Every day. Without fail. These consistent daily improvements in their physical and mental capabilities amount to tangible, significant progress over the course of many months and years.
3. They don't stop improving. They have a constant hunger for their personal development. They take advice from their coaches and mentors and action it. Immediately.
4. They visualize themselves as winners. They view themselves as heroes on the podium, with the crowd applauding them.
5. They have a growth mindset which means they are flexible enough to change gears or even complete direction, if something is not working.
6. "Procrastination" and "excuses" are not in their dictionaries. They use the word "feedback" instead of "mistake" and learn from it quickly. They don't repeat it, intentionally.
7. They meditate. Daily. Sometimes twice or multiple times a day. They strongly believe in this powerful, ancient, spiritual and sacred practice, which is now backed by numerous scientific research studies.
8. They beat their own records. They feel fulfilled when they do that.
9. They run their own race. It doesn't matter to them what others are doing. They believe in the philosophy that the only reliable and valid competition in life is with their own selves. This the actual yardstick of our own growth and personal development.

10. They are kind, honest and messengers of philanthropy. The happiness they bring to others brings even more joy, happiness and peace in their inner lives. They understand that the cause they support is much more important than their own selves.
11. They have an absolute, clear vision of their goals and missions in life.
12. They use positive words in their day-to-day lives and communication; they use "must" and "should" instead of "can't" and "won't."
13. They action positive affirmations to bring out the best in themselves. They use this tool every day and make their dreams come to fruition. They make them positive, personalized and in the present tense. They simply don't say things for the sake of saying them, but they firmly believe in it and live by it.
14. They are extremely disciplined and follow their regimes, even if they cause pain at times. However, they believe in "No pain, no gain." They are willing to sacrifice many things which they love.
15. They consider everyone and anyone as equal to their own selves. Hence, they are kind, polite and humble during conversations.
16. They have already detached themselves from a toxic ego, so the movie of themselves, other players and audience is clear to them.
17. They are truly focused and committed to accomplishing their goals.
18. Most importantly, they are not superhumans. They are average humans who have truly mastered the traits of being a champion, and to keep improving. Forever.

Story of Our response to Challenges

Once upon a time, a daughter complained to her dad. Her life was miserable, and she was overwhelmed with daily problems. She was sick of struggles all the time. It seemed as if one problem was solved, only to be followed by another. Her dad, a master chef, took her to the kitchen. He filled three pots with water and placed each on fire burners. As the three pots began to boil, he placed potatoes in one pot, eggs in the second and ground coffee beans in the third pot. He then let them sit and boil, without saying a word. His daughter waited impatiently, wondering, what her dad was doing.

After 20 minutes he turned off the burners. He took the potatoes out and placed them in a bowl. He then got the boiled eggs out and placed them in a dish. Then, he poured the coffee out and placed it in a cup. Turning to her he asked, "Honey, what can you see?"

"Potatoes, eggs, and coffee," she quickly replied. "Observe carefully," he said, "and feel the potatoes." She noticed they were soft. He asked her to take an egg and break it. After pulling off the shell, she noted the hard-boiled egg. Finally, he asked her to sip the coffee. Its rich aroma brought a smile to her face. "Dad, what does this mean?" she asked attentively. The wise dad explained, the potatoes, eggs and coffee beans each faced the same adversity – the hot boiling water. However, each responded uniquely."

The potato went in strong and hard, but in boiling water, it became soft and weak. The egg was delicate, with a thin outer shell protecting its inner yolk, until it was put in the boiling water and became tough and strong. The ground coffee beans were unique too. When exposed to the boiling water, they changed the water and created something new. "Who are you?" he asked his daughter. "When adversity knocks on your door, how do you respond? Are you a potato, an egg, or a coffee bean?"

In life, events happen around us, things happen to us, but the only thing that truly matters is what happens within us. Are we growing and becoming better than our previous selves? Are we taking on fresh challenges every day?

How do we respond to challenges and adversity?

Do we have a fixed mindset or a growth outlook?

These are important questions one should ask regularly. These are the gold standard benchmarks for any human or species. Even 0.01% progress every day is crucial, because, when made consistently over our lifetimes, it adds up and is quite significant and substantial.

Our vocabulary is highly important too. The language we speak and the words we think or write have a powerful impact on our subconscious mind. This has been proven scientifically. Using empowering words consistently changes our inner selves over a period of time. For instance, using positive-actioned affirmations improves our self-worth and motivation. "I have boundless potential. I will persevere and persist."

Mindset plays a huge role in our personality and development. Are we fixated on our ideas, feeling that a person, organization or nation is just poor and without potential? Or do we feel that everyone is unique and born with beautiful talents? Yes, everyone has shortcomings too. But are we focused on the positive qualities or do we lament the negative traits? The key lies in our understanding of ourselves and others, bringing a broader, richer perspective. The fundamental truth is that we all have infinite potential and when concentrated in the right direction, we have the energy to do almost anything we desire.

Carol Dweck, Professor of Psychology at Stanford University, through significant research explains in her book and TED talk - "A fixed mindset" assumes that our character, intelligence, and creative ability are static givens which we can't change in any meaningful way, a growth mindset thrives on challenge and sees failure "not as evidence of unintelligence but as a heartening springboard for growth and for stretching our existing abilities."

Key action steps you can apply

1. Use only positive powerful words in day to day communication. Make them your friends and use them often, e.g. solutions instead of problems, challenges instead of setbacks.
2. Avoid using words - but, won't, can't, don't. e.g.- I will do this but I can't do this (due to some excuse). I will do this and I can do this by applying (this strategy)
3. Focus only on the positive qualities of a person you interact.
4. Acknowledge and embrace imperfections in yourself and others- e.g. have the belief that you are doing your level best and *your effort matters*.

5. Enjoy the journey not the end result - e.g. have the conviction that the learning process takes time, so persevere. Plant patience.
6. Emphasize effort before talent - eg reinforcing our kids the hard work, effort and grit are the values which matter in the long scheme of life.
7. Use the word yet and not yet often- eg - say to yourself, kids, staff - "You have not mastered it yet. Your best is yet to come."

Story of Appreciation

In the olden days, when an ice cream sundae cost much less, an 8-year-old boy walked into a coffee shop and sat down at a table. A waitress put a glass of water in front of him. "How much is the ice cream sundae?" he asked. "50 cents," she replied. The little boy took his hand out of his pocket and counted the sum total of all his coins.

"How much is a plain ice cream?" he inquired. Some people were now waiting for a table and the waitress was getting a bit impatient. "35 cents," she said promptly. The little boy again counted the coins. "I'll have the plain ice cream," he said. The waitress brought the ice cream, put the bill on his table and walked away. The boy finished the ice cream, put the coins on the table and left. When the waitress came back to wipe the table, she was speechless and touched. There, just beside the empty dish, were 15 cents – her tip.

What is the key message? The cost of ice cream? The tip? Or something else? Did he complain about the cost of ice cream?

I believe it is true compliments and appreciation which matter. And they don't always have to be words, because actions speak for themselves. This little boy won the heart of the waitress because of his unexpected kindness and generosity. We all crave appreciation and compliments; but genuine praise, not flattery. The kind that comes from the core of our heart, deep from within our bellies, accompanied by a true smile from our eyes. We have the power to make an impact and influence others with true, authentic appreciation. And while we are on this subject, there are 3 Cs which are killers. I am sure you all know, but it is still worth repeating - Condemn, Complain and Criticize. Nobody likes them. Nobody. Hence, it is better to avoid doing them completely in your day-to-day life.

Key action steps you can execute

1. Practice the art of giving genuine gratitude to our loved ones, our team in our professional lives, our clients, the people who serve us - anyone.
2. Saying "Thank you" is one of the sincerest shows of appreciation you can offer anyone. These small acts of appreciation significantly boost morale, while simultaneously enhancing our happiness levels. It's a win-win habit.

Story of Stress

Once upon a time, a psychology professor was walking around in the class, teaching stress management principles to her students. As she raised a glass of water, everyone thought they'd be asked the typical "glass half empty or glass half full" question. Instead, with a smile on her face, she asked, "How heavy is this glass of water I am holding in my hand now?" Students gave answers ranging from 250-500 grams.

She replied, "From my perspective, the absolute weight of this glass doesn't really matter. It depends on how long I am holding it. If I hold it for a minute or two, it's fairly light. If I hold it for an hour straight, its weight might make my arm ache a little. If I hold it for the whole day, my arm will likely numb and may feel completely paralyzed, forcing me to drop the glass to the floor. In each scenario, the weight of the glass doesn't change, but the longer I hold it, the heavier it feels to me."

As the students nodded their heads in agreement, she remarked, "Our stresses and worries in life are very much like this glass of water. Think about them for a while and nothing happens. Think about them a little bit longer and we begin to feel sad. Think about them all day long and we will feel distressed, numb and crippled – too weak to do anything else - until we drop them."

It's vital to understand that we should let go of our stresses. No matter what happens during the day, as early as possible, we should let go of our stresses. We should not carry them through the night and into the next day with us. If we still feel the weight of yesterday's stress, it's a strong signal that we need to put the glass down. We must understand:

1. All stress is mandatory. It will happen often, whether we like it or not.
2. However, distress (a negative response to stress) is optional. We choose how we respond to specific stressful triggers.
3. Eustress (a positive response to stress) is great. Stress is part and parcel of our lives. These challenges shape us and help in our personal growth. That's how humanity has advanced and progressed over centuries and millennia. We have the conscious choice of not being in distress because it's optional. The power to respond lies with us. We can respond positively by saying to ourselves, "Yes, I can do this, and I will manage this by..." That's how we convert distress into eustress.
4. Excuses and blaming ourselves - and others - really won't take us anywhere in the grand scheme of life.

Key action steps you can execute

The underlying principle is that we all have infinite potential to change ourselves.

Once this realization happens:

1. You must develop a concrete plan to change yourself.
2. You must implement it. Action it.
3. You must act in ways which ultimately influence others.
4. You must become the change you want to see in others.

The whole process is profoundly simple, yet it isn't easy. It requires positive self-talk. Persistence in the face of adversity. Confidence that your actions will speak for themselves. Visualize yourself as a winner, as you are making progress.

Story of Happiness

Once, a group of 50 people were attending a seminar. Suddenly, the mentor stopped and decided to do a group activity. He started by giving each delegate one balloon. Everyone was asked to write their name on it using a marker pen. Then, all the balloons were collected and put in another room. Next, delegates were let into that room and asked to find the balloon which had their name written on it, within 5 minutes. Everyone was desperately searching for their named balloon, colliding into each other, pushing others and it was utter chaos. At the end of 5 minutes, no one had found their own balloon. Now, each delegate was asked to randomly collect a balloon and give it to the person whose name was written on it. Within a matter of minutes, everyone had their own balloon.

The mentor remarked, "This is exactly what is happening in our lives. Everyone seems to be crazy, searching for happiness all around, but not knowing where it is. Our happiness lies in the happiness of other people. Give them their happiness, and we will get our own happiness. This is the purpose of human life; the pursuit of happiness."

This is a powerful experiment. Newton's third law states, "For every action, there is an equal and opposite reaction." We see the application of this law in real-life situations. We speak nicely to others and they reciprocate. We speak rudely and harshly, and it is easy to imagine what will come back from the other party. The same principle applies to each and every aspect of our lives, and happiness and miracles are no exception to this rule. Just carry out simple, random acts of kindness consistently and happiness will flow around you.

It is simple, yet not easy. It requires persistent, deliberate effort at keeping the highest morale within our spouse, kids, staff, colleagues, clients, family and friends. The reality is that we often take them for granted and that is the root cause of any relationship problem. All relationships need nurturing, love and care.

Practical action steps you can perform

1. Appreciate your loved ones. Praise your spouse verbally for making daily meals for the whole family. If you find this too difficult a task, give her a gift - a bunch of flowers is great. The same principle applies to your kids. They need the right direction and appropriate praise. Stickers will do most of the time. There's no need to buy fancy, expensive gadgets.
2. In a business setting, have a chat or laugh with your team over a cup of tea or coffee. Take a step further and make it for them. The love you get from these simple acts is immense and improves the business atmosphere and staff morale. It breeds an important element of equality and trust.

3. Make a list of all team members' birth dates. Celebrate together with a piece of cake. Give them a small gift if you are the "boss". It is a no-brainer. Everyone loves the fact that they are loved and appreciated. It only takes 20-25 minutes and the rewards are immense. The fact that a team member gets a lower salary doesn't mean that they have a smaller role in an organization.
4. There are many other ways to praise and you can make your own list, but you get the point.

Story of Forgiveness and Acceptance

It was a cold night in February 2007 when the car holding Chris Williams and his family was hit by a 17-year-old drunk driver. Immediately, Chris checked on his children in the back seat and quickly realized his 11-year-old son and 9-year-old daughter had died. Then, he watched as his pregnant wife, who was sitting next to him, exhaled for the last time. Meanwhile, Chris was in so much pain he could barely move his arm to turn off his car engine. However, before he had even been rescued from his car, Williams told the media he had had this thought: "Whoever has done this to us - I forgive them. I don't care what the circumstances were; I forgive them." He proved as good as his word, going on to publicly forgive his family's killer and developing a relationship with him and his family.

Today, Williams is a motivational speaker, sharing his incredible story of healing and forgiveness and inspiring others to extend mercy and forgiveness as well. "This is my experience with forgiveness; letting go, moving forward, and being healed. What burden could you lay at the Lord's feet, today, that He might be allowed to work miracles in your life?" Forgiving someone doesn't mean that their behavior was okay. What it does mean is that we are ready to move on. To release the heavy weight.

To shape our own lives, on our terms, without any unnecessary burdens.

Mo Gawdat is the Chief Business Officer at Google X and responsible for some of the company's boldest projects, such as self-driving cars and a balloon-powered global internet. Before he joined Google and working as a stock trader in Dubai, he used his engineer's mindset to create an "equation for happiness". The equation says that your happiness is greater than, or equal to, your perception of the events in your life, minus your expectation of how life should be.

When his 21-year-old son, Ali, died during a routine operation, Gawdat turned to the equation, which they had worked on together, as a radical act of acceptance and moving on. Mo's book, "Solve for Happy: Engineer your Path to Joy," explains the theories underpinning the equation and how it helped him sustain his life after Ali's death. Mo has set himself a target of making 10 million people happy and hopes that his readers will set themselves a target of 25 people each, or more, depending on their reach.

What Williams did was an extreme act of mercy to such a tragic catastrophe. This is certainly extremely challenging, even for a very kind person. However, knowing what Williams did, is certainly an inspiring story for those who have experienced such circumstances, or are suffering from bereavement now - or for those who may experience such events in the future. Mo's story underpins how a bereaved family can turn a highly tragic event into a life of purpose.

Every human being in such situations goes through phases of denial, anger, grief, depression and acceptance - not always in the same sequence. It is normal to feel these human emotions as they make us uniquely human. We all are unique, and some people can remain in a state of anger and denial for prolonged periods. Some can experience grief and depression for many years and sometimes decades. They cannot forgive themselves and hence cannot move on with their lives. The only way forward in such tragic circumstances is *Acceptance*. This is the only point where healing and rehabilitation begins. Ultimately, there is a phase of finding meaning and purpose even after losing one's loved ones.

Practical action steps you can implement

If you are going through such tragic events in your life, find out which stage you are in. Being in the first 4 stages for a few months is normal. It is only when you are stuck in the stages of grief and depression beyond many months or years, that there is a problem. It is vital that you seek help from your family and friends and also from trained professionals; for example, bereavement counsellors, compassionate psychologists, and your local general practitioner.

Story of heart

My 7-year-old son was doing some preparation for the Spellodrome competition at his school. I was helping him remember the spellings. For some reason, he was stuck and was not able to remember the spelling of "heart." I told him, "Son, it's simple; how would you spell "hear," like "Can you hear me?" He was aware of the spelling of "hear" so he pronounced it correctly. "Now you just have to add the letter "t" to it. Simple." From then onwards, he could spell "heart" correctly. I smiled, but for a different reason. Interestingly, the word "heart" is spelt h-ear-t with the "ear" exactly in the middle. Even more interesting is the fact that our two human ears, when put together, very much resemble our physical heart.

What is the purpose of this simple story? Just at that moment, it dawned on me that the only way to win a person's heart is by hearing them. It is a highly effective skill which is especially relevant in the modern world, where there is so much distraction. The overwhelming majority of us in the world today are engrossed in their devices and screens. Even when people are having lunch or dinner outside, or sitting in a cafeteria, we see them just gazing at their screens as if they can't just sit down and have food or a chat. If they are driving, they are chatting - or worse; getting angry at someone on their Bluetooth.

We, as a society, are becoming social media and technology addicts to a significant extent, and this problem is increasing rapidly. We really don't need any research to prove this. You can find this problem wherever you go, from bus stops, to schools, shopping malls, restaurants and, most worryingly, at our homes. The only way forward is deep listening. If we add the elements of empathy and compassion together, it is like a cherry on the cake.

We all crave active deep listening. Someone who can listen to us. Really hear us. Beyond oneself. Beyond any personal gains or agenda. Once we are able to achieve this, then you can imagine the world with really sociable people who chat face-to-face and interact with one another. So, what should you do?

Key action steps you can apply

1. No phones or screens during family lunches or dinners. It is ironic that we have to reinforce this although it is so very obvious. Just imagine 20-25 years ago, when we all used to have our family dinners with smiles and laughter!
2. No screens (e.g. TV, mobiles, iPads etc.) at least 2 hours before bedtime. Studies show that our sleep is significantly better by adopting this good habit!
3. Have a good chat with all family members during meal times. It is one of the most important Quadrant 2 activities.
4. Really, actively listen to your friend or client. No interruptions. Only smile and use follow-up questions. You will be surprised as to how much the other person can speak, even if they are complete introverts.

5. Open body language and gestures invite people to open up.
6. Use Silence. It is one of the most powerful yet most underutilized communication tools. It has been eloquently put that you must only speak if the power of words is more than silence. Experiment using gestures, such as smiles and silence, and keep to simple, concise, yet powerful words when chatting. The effects are immense.

Story of Growing Fire in your Belly

We once went camping on a weekend at the height of winter, when the temperature was in single digits. It was an adventure with my close friend and our two kids, aged 6 and 8. It was a sort of glamping as we were new to camping and most of our needs were catered for. We still have to keep the inside of the tent warm by constantly burning wood at regular intervals, though. We made warm tea on the burner and played board games; it was a lot of fun. Both my friend and I decided to have a campfire just outside our tents. Our kids were excited, as they were keen to have toasted marshmallows.

Our host gave us all the ingredients that one could ever need. We had the designated platform to light the fire, some large and medium logs of wood, some kindling and a match. We were new to the business of making a campfire. It was really cold and very windy that evening. We all had our thermals and jackets on. The kids were wanted to help, so they pulled the heavy trolley of wood to the tent area. My friend had some experience with fire, so we decided to start. We put down kindling as a base, then the larger logs just on top of them. My friend lit the fire with a match. It started, but after just a couple of minutes, it went out. We repeated the process a few times and ended with the same result. Something was not right. The small flames were just not strong enough to burn the medium or big logs of wood. We decided that we definitely needed to have much more kindling to keep a sustained fire before we could add bigger bits of wood.

The kids were excited, and they gathered good amounts of twigs, bark and leaves from all around our tent area. We put all our effort into getting this raw material first. We had no formal training in lighting a campfire, but I believe this was the most crucial step. We made a sort of pyramid of all the collected material in the center and put some small pieces of wood on the periphery. We lit this material first and then, hooray! The intensity of fire was much better this time. It was really windy, so we wasted no time in putting some medium logs first and then larger pieces of wood on top of it. We had done it; the campfire

was raging, and the kids were jubilant. We sat around on chairs and had a lovely time with lots of chat. Kids and grown-ups alike enjoyed the freshly toasted marshmallows.

I reflected later on and realized that any small or big projects in our lives are like campfires. They all start with an idea. We have to constantly fuel an idea and keep our passion alive by doing small, daily acts. These small yet important improvements keep the fire in our bellies alive. Only when our inner fire is mature enough, can we add more challenges. And that's how we grow...

To simplify:

> Dream big... (The Bold projects/ Big picture (big logs of wood) of your life)
> Start small... (The small daily wins (smaller blocks of wood)
> Fuel it up... (Passion (the fire in your belly) - twigs, bark, paper - the kindling)
> Act Now... (Make your idea come alive (light the fire)

Story of beginning with the end in mind. Enjoy the Ride.

Please read this-

Aoccdrnig to a rseearch at Cmabrigde Uinervtisy, it deosn't mttaer in waht oredr the ltteers in a wrod are, the olny iprmoatnt tihng is taht the frist and lsat ltteer be at the rghit pclae. The rset can be a toatl mses and you can sitll raed it wouthit porbelm. Tihs is bcuseae the huamn mnid deos not raed ervey lteter by istlef, but the wrod as a wlohe.

This study shows how our brain works in understanding words as a whole, as long as we register the first and last letters correctly. Metaphorically, it signifies the journey of our wonderful lives. We all have many challenges in our daily life; some small, some big and some in between.

This story glorifies the fact that we will reach our mission in life if we internalize:

1. We have a clear starting point for our vision, goal and purpose.
2. We take immediate action.
3. We consistently work on our projects.

4. The journey can be chaotic and unpredictable.
5. Higher forces of the universe will work for us.
6. We achieve our mission, our higher purpose - something much bigger than us.

The road map to success in our lives is quite similar to this study.
Lean your ladder against the right wall.
Have absolute clarity of purpose.
Take actionable steps.
Starting an important project is a brave first step.
Boldness (not arrogance) is the hallmark of a genius.
Enjoy the journey.
Have a clear vision and well-defined goals.
There will be many challenges and obstacles during our ride.
There will be many struggles during our adventure.
We will reach our project goal.
The momentum we gain will help us succeed in even more challenging projects ahead.

Introduction to MASTERS

If we read a book just for the sake of reading, nothing will change.

Only appropriate actions lead to desirable results.

There are steps to achieving our desired goals in any aspects of life- family, friends, health, work, finances, fun, spiritual. It is utmost vital to follow the principles which are time tested and so precious - there are no doubts. Only positivity and abundance flows.

1. Clarity of goals - This is the most important step. It requires deep reflection and introspection. It is based on our values and our purpose in life. It requires tools and habits which help us connect with our subconscious mind. This help us lead a life with a deep meaningful purpose as ultimately it will give us sustained enduring happiness. There are simply no shortcuts. It is based on sound simple daily practices which anyone can develop.
2. Core values - are the foundation pillars of what we stand for. Everyone should take time and effort to declare his/her own core values. They are the fundamental beliefs of a person or an organization. These principles guide behaviour and help us understand the difference between right and

wrong. They also help us in determining if we are on the right path and help fulfill our goals by creating a positive guiding force. Some good examples are -

Confidence	Honesty
Pleasing personality	Efficiency
Enthusiasm	Innovation
Passion	Creativity
Lifelong learning	Good humor
Focussedness	Compassion
Politeness	Spirit of adventure
Humility	Motivation
Respectful	Positivity
Perseverance	Optimism
Team player	Fitness
Reliability	Courage
Loyalty	Education
Commitment	Patriotism
Open-mindedness	Altruism
Consistency	Environmentalism

3. Purpose or meaning of life -

The purpose of life is a life of purpose.

— *Robert Byrne*

We all want to be happy, but are we exactly clear how? Hence writing our singular purpose of life is so deeply important. It requires deep thought, introspection and then formulating one singular purpose of life. It is based on our core values and what we want to do with our lives. It is a one or two sentence statement. It is ultimately a strong guiding force to our lives. A clear definite purpose is a meaningful goal which connects us with other fellow humans. Viktor Frankl wrote in his book *Man's Search for Meaning*, " this fundamental need for purpose and direction may be as important to our psychological growth as eating is to our biological survival."

Without a clear *why*, we don't exactly know what to do or how best to do it. The good news is we all can tap into a *clear why* by following MASTERS - habits which are so powerful and time tested that we just simply see us transforming miraculously. They are all incredibly simple practices. The key, however is, consistency of daily actions. They can be tapped from all bountiful sources of mother nature.

We can define our core values and purpose more effectively if we have a structured framework set on strong principles. This brings us to the 7 daily habits to transform ourselves and leading a life we all desire. These 7 habits truly make us the

"**MASTERS**" of our own destiny and the champion of our lives.

These are

> **M** - Meditation and Mindfulness
> **A** - Affirmations (positive, present, personalized and Actioned)
> **S** - Smile + Silence
> **T** - Thinking (Reflection) + Thanking (Gratitude)
> **E** - Exercise (Physical)
> **R** - Reading
> **S** - Story Sharing + Scribbling (Writing)

This is best achieved by writing on our journal or notebook. No written goals mean no clear instructions to our subconscious mind and hence vague goals only. They should be set as high as possible. We know that setting a high goal and reaching to some extent is far better than setting a mediocre goal and achieving it completely. Eg- Setting up a small business is a worthy goal but dreaming and actioning of making it international is truly amazing. We may not become global in the end but perhaps become a national organization. Finally working towards it- small steps daily is a beautiful piece of artwork.

Mindfulness and Meditation →
MASTERS

"Our life is shaped by our mind,
for we become what we think."
— *Buddha*

"The best way to capture moments is to pay attention.
This is how we cultivate mindfulness."
— *Jon Kabat-Zinn.*

"Everyone of us already has the seed of mindfulness.
The practice is to cultivate it."
— *Thich Nhat Hanh*

"The mind is just like a muscle- the more you exercise it,
the stronger it gets and the more it can expand."
— *Idowu Koyenikan*

Mindfulness is a universal, modern tool to enhance our lives. The ancient practice of meditation makes us calmer, more balanced and improve our well being. Jon Kabat-Zinn, a world authority on the use of mindfulness training defines it as: "Paying attention in a particular way: on purpose, in the present moment, and non-judgmentally."- Mindfulness is a mental state of openness, awareness and focus, and meditation is just one way amongst hundreds of learning to cultivate this state. It is a modern practice that involves paying full attention to our experiences- good or bad- it is not a state of tantric bliss and has no religious dimensions.

Mindfulness is

- Recognizing emotions as they come without becoming charged.
- Identifying ourselves as we truly are -not linking with feelings or mistakes.
- Living more in the Now and less in the past or future.
- Tool to cultivate happiness available to everyone.

However mindfulness is not -

- Emptying the mind or removing thoughts as they come.
- A relaxation exercise, though it will make us more relaxed eventually.
- An escape strategy from own personality, it reveals who we really are.
- A tool to live life without planning - we can still plan in a mindful way.

Listing the benefits of mindfulness is like quantifying love, and misses the essence. However, there has been a significant scientific research and they are relevant in all aspects of life-

Thinking
- Improved memory
- Faster response times
- Improved Mental skills
- Improved Focus
- Improved decision making
- Enhanced gut instincts

Health
- Reduced anxiety
- Strong immune system
- Reduced pain levels
- Reduction of stress levels
- Reduced depressive thinking
- Improved sleep
- Well functioning health
- Good overall health

Happiness
- Higher self esteem
- Improved self-confidence
- Increased satisfaction from work
- Improved relationships
- Unlocking untapped potential
- Heightened focus on goals

Life skills
- Improved communication
- Improved listening skills
- Increased compassion
- Improved self-awareness
- Mastery on our emotions
- Improved emotional intelligence
- Increased resilience in adversity

How to Meditate

The following meditation exercise is an excellent introduction to the beginners and as you progress, feel free to add new techniques.

1. Sit on a chair with a straight back. Relax your shoulders and neck. You can sit on the floor if you prefer.
2. Gently close your eyes.
3. Simply breathe naturally. Make no efforts to control the breath.
4. Focus your attention on the breath (the anchor) and how our chest and belly moves with each inhalation and exhalation.
5. If your mind wanders and thoughts come, acknowledge them and go back to your anchor- your breath.

Practical action you can execute

1. Do it daily -Meditation is a practice you can do anytime, anywhere. Avoid thinking that you can't meditate. It is simple and there is no such thing as a good or bad meditation.
2. Cultivate a habit - Like any new habit it may seem difficult at first, but over a period of time it becomes a key part of our daily routine.
3. Start simple - Meditation is not a complex practice. There is no need for any special tool. Beginners may worry whether they are doing it right or not and pay too much emphasis on the technique. Thoughts will come and go during the practice and our aim is to acknowledge them and return to our breath.
4. Start small and build up - Begin with just 1-2 mins and gradually build to 5,10,20 minutes and so on. Do not worry too much if you miss a session due to some urgency.
5. Meditate in the morning - as the richness and benefits of this exercise stays throughout the day.
6. Be patient- as the benefits start showing gradually over a period of 6-12 weeks.
7. Get mentors - and seek guidance from experienced instructors or download free guided apps like smiling minds or paid ones like calm or headspace.
8. Remember the proven benefits - as it will help you continue the practice.
9. Meditation is not a magic wand - it doesn't remove challenges and doesn't guarantee, we will be successful in all our projects or goals. When times are good, everything may feel fine, but it is when we are feeling down and depressed that we need help. The mental toughness we get from meditation enables us to bounce forwards.
10. Consistency is the key - do it again. Daily.

Affirmations → MASTERS

Daily affirmations are simple, positive statements declaring specific goals in their completed states. Although they sound quite simple, these highly empowering remarks have profound effects on our subconscious mind. Affirmations are our daily interactions with the subconscious mind. They help us stay focused on our goals and to come up with solutions to any problem in our life. They also create higher vibes for happiness, joy, appreciation, and gratitude.

The daily habit of positive affirmations eliminates bombardment of negative thoughts and beliefs. To achieve this, we must enrich our subconscious mind with positive thoughts and images of the new reality we wish to harness. There are important guidelines for creating smart positive affirmations (PA). The simple magic formula is

PA = 4 P X A

1. **P**ersonalized
2. **P**resent tense
3. **P**ositive vibes
4. **P**urpose
5. **A**ctioned

Action is the key in positive affirmations. Simply saying with positivity, purpose and all visualization won't work if we don't act on them.

Practical Action steps you can implement

1. We must write them down.
2. Making affirmations for us, not others.
3. Starting with the words - " I am.. ", " I have "," I believe "
4. Use only the present tense.
5. State only the positive. No negative words allowed.
6. Keep it simple and concise.
7. Make it specific.
8. Include an action word ending with –ing. Eg enjoying, working, learning.
9. Include powerful emotions and feeling words
10. Include your purpose of life.
11. Action it immediately.

List of positive feeling Emotions-

We must add " I am …."

1. Confident
2. Loving
3. Smiling
4. Enthusiastic
5. Passionate
6. Grateful
7. Kind
8. Compassionate
9. Motivated
10. Perseverant
11. Comfortable
12. Focussed
13. Committed
14. Decisive
15. Inspired
16. Miraculous
17. Magnetic
18. Humble
19. Optimistic
20. Relaxed
21. Resilient
22. Vibrant
23. Beautiful
24. Wise
25. Zestful

Some examples of powerful positive affirmations -

I inspire my kids to fully manifest their unique strengths.

I am a perfect role model for my family.

I am confidently delivering my first TED talk to an audience of over 1,000 people and getting a standing ovation.

I am attracting joy, love and peace in my life.

I am confidently expressing myself genuinely with humility.

I am feeling enthusiastic.

I am passionate about my mission.

I am a lifelong student and learning every day.

I am effectively conveying warm wishes to my loving spouse.

I am genuinely happy knowing- I have made a difference to my clients life.

I am the master of my soul and the captain of my ship.

Practical tips and strategies

1. **Timing** - Positive Affirmations can be done anytime of the day. Morning is usually the best as it sets the tone for the whole day. What matters most is that we do it consistently. During challenging times this is one of our greatest friend.
2. **Method** - PA can be done with eyes open or closed. It can be done silently or loudly depending on personal situation.
3. **Emotions** - Saying them with full conviction, certainty with utmost authenticity is highly empowering.
4. **Visualizing** - them with full emotions, colours and images in the mind is most definitely powerful.

5. **Combination** - Good news for multi-taskers. It can be combined with daily exercise at home or gym, provided we keep ourselves *safe*. The effect of PA + exercise is synergistic. The good effects of these two activities are much more than its sum.
6. **Frequency** - PA is best done daily or even more. It will always bring positivity and goodness in life even when times are smooth. However, doing once a day is better than not practising at all.
7. **Length** - PA are ideally simple, short sentences as they are easier for our mind to remember and repeat.
8. **Number** - PA can usually range between 5-20, depending on the time one can devote.
9. **Duration** - can range between 1-4 minutes, again depending on the number of affirmations you have chosen.

Smile → MASTERS

If you have to implement only one idea of this book- Please Smile and read this chapter.

> **"Let us always meet each other with smile,
> for the smile is the beginning of love"**
> — *Mother Teresa*

> **"Because of your smile, you make life more beautiful."**
> — *Thich Nhat Hanh*

> **"Too often we underestimate the power of a touch,
> a smile, a kind word, a listening ear,
> a honest compliment, or the smallest act of caring,
> all of which have the potential to turn a life around."**
> — *Leo Buscaglia*

> **"Beauty is power; a smile is its sword."**
> — *John Ray*

> **"Peace begins with a smile."**
> — *Mother Teresa*

> **"The greatest self is a peaceful smile,
> that always sees the world smiling back.**
> — *Bryant H. McGill*

"A warm smile is the universal language of kindness."
— William A. Ward

We all know that laughter is the best medicine. But laughter's quiet cousin, the smile also improve our health and wellbeing and the people around us.

Some Science about Smiles

1. Simulating a genuine smile can boost our mood. Psychologists have found that even if we are in a bad mood, we can instantly lift our spirits by simulating a genuine smile.
2. Smile boosts our immune system. Our body is more relaxed when we smile, which contributes to good health and a stronger immune system.
3. Smiles are infectious. In a Swedish study, people had difficulty frowning when they looked at other subjects who were smiling, and their facial muscles arranged into smiles all on their own.
4. Smile relieve stress. Our body instantly releases endorphins (the good positive hormones) when we smile, even when we really don't want to smile !
5. Smiling is a universal sign of happiness. While hand shakes, hugs and bows all have different meanings across cultures, smiling is known worldwide and in all diverse cultures as a signal of happiness and acceptance.
6. Smiling at work significantly improves our relationships with our clients and colleagues and ultimately makes the working environment much relaxed.
7. A genuine smile uses 12 facial muscles as compared to a frown which uses 11 muscles. This extra 1 percent effort put in a genuine smile has far-reaching great consequences compared to a frown.

8. Babies are born with the ability to smile. They learn a lot of behaviors and sounds from watching the people around them. Even blind babies smile.
9. Smiling helps us get promoted. Smile makes a person more attractive, sociable, confident and most likely to get promoted.
10. Smiles are the most easily recognizable facial expression. People can recognize smiles even from a far distance.
11. Women smile more than men. Men should learn from women.
12. Smiles are more attractive than makeup. A research study conducted by Orbit Complete discovered that 69% of people find women more attractive when they smile than when they are wearing makeup.
13. There are 19 different types of smiles as per UC-San Francisco researchers and categorized into - polite "social" smiles which engage fewer muscles, and sincere "felt" smiles that use more muscles on both sides of the face.

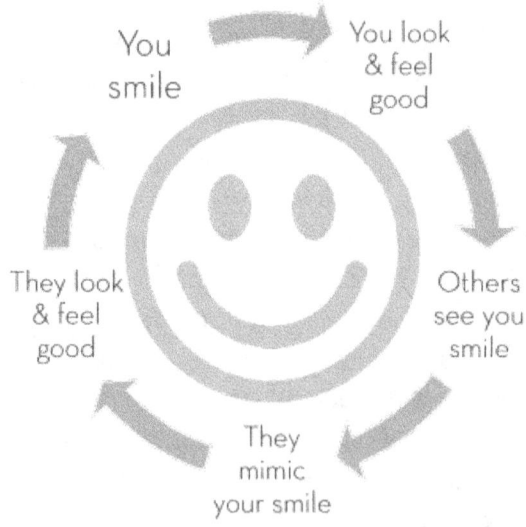

Positive cycle of Smiling

Practical strategies you can execute

1. Practice Smiling. Do it right now. Put a big, warm smile on your face. Not a fake smile- rather a real genuine smile, like you are seeing a good old friend after many years. An authentic smile brings shine in your eyes and develops crow's feet on the sides of eyes. Now, think of some negative situation in your life, but keep smiling. It is difficult to hold an unhappy thought in our mind while keeping a smile on our face.
2. Give Yourself a smile nudge. The trick is to smile as you go through your day. You will need a cue to smile often - "smile cue." You may choose a sound as a reminder, like a phone ringing or an email notification or visual cue like seeing someone laughing. You may put a sticker on your computer saying - "Make your smiles count."Smile every time you encounter these cues.
3. Stay Motivated. People who smile while talking make a great impression because they look more confident and friendly. You can even "hear" a smile over the phone. Smile when taking a phone call and you will notice better connections with the person on the other side.
4. Keep your smiles natural, warm, and sincere. You are simply trying to cultivate an elevated mood. Even just a small, almost faint smile can elevate your mood.
5. Smile every time you think of it, not only when you notice your smile cue.
6. Think of something you really like when you smile – it will help make your smile sincere eg- your favourite holiday destination or meeting an old friend.
7. Take a deep breath when you smile. It increases the relaxation and mood-enhancing power of smiling.

8. Place notes and reminders everywhere eg- home, office to remind you to smile more. Put a note on the phone, send yourself an email, or make a note on your calendar. Make sure you have plenty of reminders to smile often. Eventually, it will become your most beautiful and cherished jewel.
9. Take smiling to the next level - laughing. Laughing out loud- like smiling, creates an emotional state that relieves stress and elevates your mood. Eg-read good jokes, watch funny movies and talk to jolly people. Think of the funniest stories you know and tell your family, staff and clients.
10. You can smile at your own silly mistakes, at your imperfections. In fact, you can laugh at them. This is a sign of maturity and will take you to yet another higher level.

Silence → MASTERS

> "Silence is the best answer for all questions... and Smiling is the best reaction to all situations..."

> "It is better in prayer to have a heart without words than words without a heart."
> — *Mahatma Gandhi*

> "Keep silence for the most part, and speak only when you must, and then briefly."
> — *Epictetus*

> "Silence is sometimes the best answer."
> — *Dalai Lama*

> "In the end, we will remember not the words of our enemies, but the silence of our friends."
> — *Martin Luther King Jr.*

We live in a loud world where TV, music, and smartphones fill our lives. Silence and solitude are luxuries today. We are constantly bombarded by technology as we call, text, and email to feel less lonely. However, how often do we take the time to sit and relish the silence and doing nothing? Yes, doing nothing. Silence gives us space to deep thinking in our subconscious minds. It is very healthy for our physical and mental wellbeing. It's time to go to our quiet and peaceful place, and feed our mind and body.

So, why should we be silent? Here are some important benefits backed by scientific research.

1. **We become calmer,** less prone to negative thinking or influenced by negative emotions. When we are at peace in a state of calm, we note what really works and what doesn't in our life. Hence, when we practice silence, we tend to be more successful than others who don't.
2. **Boosts our gut instincts** - When we are alone, we are not really alone. We actually strike a conversation with ourselves. In a way, we engage in self-talk. We are listening to the self. The more time we spend alone in silent mode, the better is our intuition. Ultimately it improves self-trust.
3. **Understand us better** - "Knowing others is intelligence; knowing yourself is true wisdom. Mastering others is strength; mastering yourself is true power." - Lao Tzu. By practicing silence, we know our innate potential, strength, passion and accomplish extraordinary results. We leverage our strengths and help counteract our weaknesses.
4. **Heightened awareness** - How do we know that we are traveling on the right path? Silence improves our conscience.
5. **Cultivates Creativity** - Studies have shown that when we are in silent mode, we engage more with our mind and bring its deep untapped creative powers to surface. It is said that one day Sir Newton was taking a rest in silence and relaxing under an apple tree in the garden. All of a sudden, an apple fell on his head and made him discover gravity. Silence boosts our creativity and imagination.

6. **Reduces** our daily stress and all problems linked to it.
7. **Plant patience** - Studies have shown that people who are more in silent mode tend to have more patience. This is extremely relevant in today's fast-paced world. Imagine getting stuck in traffic congestion, most people easily get angry and show reckless attitudes. Can we reach our destination quickly by this? A far better option is just to be silent or perhaps listen to music or audiobooks or radio.
8. **Widens our vision and perspective** - Einstein said, "Logic will get you from A to B. Imagination will take you everywhere." Problems and challenges will always appear in different shapes and forms. Silence helps us to view them from a unique perspective. and we are better able to manage any situation.
9. **Discover our true calling** - Most people today have no idea what they want to do in their lives. They are usually distracted by other people's opinion and neglect their own true calling or purpose of life. In silence, we listen to our inner voice. It is a great habit to discover our life plan.
10. **Increased focus and attention.**
11. **Cultivate beautiful relationships with our loved ones** - family, friends, staff and clients. It is far better to stay quiet with a smiling face than to say something which may ruin a relationship.
12. **Silence → Grow will power → Improved discipline → Success**
13. **Improves decision making in life.**
14. **Grows our brain** - Silence can grow our brain cells and slow the rate of aging. A study on mice has shown that two hours of silence each day can lead to the development of new brain cells. When our brain is developing with more engaging activities, it will age slower. Hence, silence is

important to our mental health and can prevent depression and dementia.

15. **Restores our balance** and bring mind and body in harmony. Most people tend to be living in a hurry and forget to spend the time to nurture their spiritual self. To grow, we need to pause, reflect on our life and observe events happening around us. We need a broader, bigger perspective and ensure we are traveling on the right path. It is similar to climbing a ladder against a wall. Not any wall, but the wall of our true purpose. Only if it is leaning against the right wall, we reach our desired destination.

16. **Attain higher emotional balance** - We are likely to get less angry, less prone to the barrage of negative emotions, and achieve more mental stability. This is highly crucial in the modern world where multiple distractions, stress, and pressures are always trying to get a hold of us. Silence is the ultimate gift and solution.

Practical Action steps

1. Find a quiet place where you are peaceful and comfortable.
2. You can choose to sit or walk around as long as you are relaxed.
3. Just stay in silence, focus only on your breath. Avoid the temptation of doing any work during this period.
4. Just spending 10 minutes a day in silence will work wonders.
5. If you do not have 10 mins, start with 1 minute only and gradually build up.
6. Never give up, as consistency is the key to any good habit.
7. The benefits will start coming in a few weeks time.

Thinking → MASTERS

"Education is not the learning of facts,
but the training of the mind to think."
— *Albert Einstein*

"A person is but the product of their thoughts.
What they think, they become."
— *Mahatma Gandhi*

"Educating the mind without educating
the heart is no education at all."
— *Aristotle*

THINK before you speak

- **T** - Is it **T**rue?
- **H** - Is it **H**elpful?
- **I** - Is it **I**nspiring?
- **N** - Is it **N**ecessary?
- **K** - Is it **K**ind?

"The real man smiles in trouble, gathers strength
from distress, and grows brave by reflection."
— *Thomas Paine*

Introspection or self-reflection can be described as examining our own internal thoughts and feelings and reflecting on what they mean.

Benefits of Self-Reflection

We have over 50,000 thoughts per day, over half of which are negative and over 90% of them are just repeated from yesterday (Wood, 2013). Only utilizing our time properly, we give ourselves the opportunity to grow and develop. Enhancing our ability to understand ourselves and our motivations and learn more about our own values helps us take the power away from the distractions of our modern, fast-paced life, and bring our focus back where it belongs (Wood, 2013).

Practical action steps you can implement

1. Self-reflection exercises are best done when we are in silent mode- which means that there is no or minimal distraction from the outside world.
2. One practical way is to do Naikan exercise. The word Naikan is a Japanese term and literally means *looking inside*. It was originally developed by a Japanese man Ishin Yoshimoto (1916-88). It is a structured exercise in which we ask 3 important questions centred around key people in our lives
   - *What I had received from that person?*
   - *What I had given to that person?*
   - *What troubles or difficulties I had caused to that person ?*
3. Examining our own life is profoundly sensible and simple, yet not easy.

4. It must be done consistently like any good habit. If you can not do it daily - schedule it on a weekly or fortnightly basis. The benefits are immense.
5. If you do not prefer Naikan for any reason- the following questions are great ways to get you in a self-reflecting mode
    - Am I utilizing my time wisely?
    - Am I taking anyone or anything for granted?
    - Am I applying a fresh, healthy perspective?
    - Am I living genuinely to my true self?
    - Am I waking up in the morning ready to take on fresh challenges?
    - Am I thinking positive thoughts before I sleep?
    - Am I putting good effort into my relationships?
    - Am I looking after myself physically?
    - Am I achieving the goals I've set for myself?
    - Who am I really?
    - If I had to instill one piece of advice in my kids' mind, what would that be?
    - What truly matters most in my life? Why?
    - What am I going to do about the issues that matter most in my life?
    - Have I done anything recently worth remembering?
    - Have I made someone smile today?
    - Have I given up on anything? Why?
    - Does it really matter what others think about me?
    - When did I last push the confines of my comfort zone?
    - What random act of kindness have I experienced that I will never forget?
    - How shall I live now, knowing I will die?
    - What's the one thing I'd like others to remember about me at the end of my life?

Thanking → MASTERS

"It is not happiness that brings us gratitude.
It's gratitude that brings us happiness."

"Thank you is the best prayer that anyone could say.
I say that one a lot. Thank you expresses extreme
gratitude, humility, understanding."

— *Alice Walker*

" I am grateful for the challenges that
helped me grow into the person I am today."

" Gratitude is the healthiest of all human emotions.
The more you express gratitude for what you have,
the more likely you have even more to express
gratitude for."

— *Zig Ziglar*

"Be grateful for today and never take anything
for granted. Life is a blessing."

"God gave you 86400 seconds today.
Have you used one to say thank you?"

— *William A. Ward*

> "Develop an attitude of gratitude, and give thanks for everything that happens to you, knowing that every step forward is a step towards achieving something bigger and better than your current situation."
>
> — Brian Tracy

> "A grateful heart is a magnet for miracles."

Benefits of gratitude

There is an enormous degree of research done on gratitude, all of which show profound benefits. It makes us happier. 5 minute per day of gratitude journaling or simple prayer can increase our long-term well-being by more than 10 percent. Exactly similar response as doubling our income!

How does it happen?

We practice gratefulness → We become happier → We make everyone around us happier → This gives us happiness → We make gratitude our daily habit.

So what is the root problem?

We take everyone and everything for granted. It begins with our loved ones - spouses, kids, parents, staff, colleagues, etc. Then comes the daily commodities which we feel we are entitled to eg all the material goods that we can think of. Eg- a pizza delivery girl/ boy arrives 5-10 mins late, we may feel unappreciative and now a days the competition is so strong that we may get a complete refund of our order if the pizza is late by a certain time. This is ridiculous. Instead of being grateful to the delivery person and the whole process we are in a complaint mode. This brings us to a state of being ungrateful and unhappy. The solution to this common problem is cultivating a gratefulness habit. Being appreciative of simple small things is highly important.

1. Gratitude makes us more reliable, social and affectionate. Hence, it helps us make more friends, deepen our relationships, and improve our marriage.
2. Gratitude is strongly linked with optimism. It makes us happy, improves our overall health and has been shown to increase lifespan by at least a few years.
3. Gratitude transform us an efficient organizer, help us network, increases our decision-making skills, our productivity and help us get mentors. Hence, it helps us achieve career goals and make our workplace friendly and enjoyable.
4. Gratitude reduces materialism which is linked with low well-being and increased mental health disorder. There's no problem wanting more. The main question is *why*? The problem with materialism is that it makes people feel less competent, reduces feelings of connections, shortens our ability to appreciate the richness in life, generates negative emotions, and makes us more self-centered. Fortunately, there is so much of minimalism revolution going globally that is worth trying it for a couple of months. Check website of Joshua Fields and Ryan Nicodemus at the minimalists.com
5. Gratitude helps us cultivate empathy and compassion. The happiness we give to others due to these selfless acts exponentially increases our happiness levels. We become more kind and friendly.
6. Gratitude helps us becoming more generous and charitable. These kind acts bring us deep, meaningful and sustained happiness.
7. Gratitude improves sleep quality, reduces the time required to fall asleep, increases sleep duration and thus help with insomnia.

8. Gratitude keeps you away from me (doctor). It leads to better coping skills, managing terminal conditions like cancer and HIV, faster recovery from certain medical procedures, positive changes in our immunity. Research suggests- people engaging in gratitude practices feel less pain, go to the doctor less often, have lower blood pressure, and less likely to develop a mental disorder.
9. Gratitude helps us bounce forward. We become more proactive, ask for help when we need and more likely to grow during challenges.
10. Gratefulness helps us network. It helps us getting mentored. When we are grateful, we are more likely to help others and become their mentors. It is a two way street and we remain appreciative of the love and learning from others and vice versa.

Practical action steps you can implement

1. It may sound simplistic yet immensely powerful. Saying "thank you" with genuine gratefulness reflecting from our gestures and tone of voice is the best thing we can do. This "thank you" can be showered to anyone anytime.
2. Make a habit of saying thank you at least 5 times everyday. The more you do it, the better it is for your happiness levels.
3. A simple prayer to thank all your loved ones daily is a great start of the day.
4. Write 5 thank you sentences in your journal every morning or night. Believe me, it takes only a couple of minutes per day and the rewards are marvellous.
5. Cultivate this elegant habit and practice it like a champion.

Exercise → MASTERS

> "To enjoy the glow of good health,
> you must exercise."
>
> — Gene Tunney

> "Take care of your body.
> It's the only place you have to live."
>
> — Jim Rohn

> "Work hard (exercise) in silence.
> Let your success be your noise."

> "You can feel sore tomorrow,
> or you can feel sorry tomorrow. You choose."

Exercise is the physical exertion of the body - making the body do a physical activity which results in a level of physical fitness and mental health. It aims to maintain or enhance our physical fitness and general health. There are three intensities -

- Light exercise - eg light walk.
- Moderate exercise - makes you slightly short of breath. eg-walking briskly, cycling moderately or walking up a hill.
- Vigorous exercise - pushing the body to its limit eg- running, fast cycling, and heavy weight training.

3 main categories of exercise

1. Aerobic eg- brisk walking, jogging,
2. Anaerobic- lifting heavy weights.
3. Agility training or Sports: eg- tennis, badminton, squash

Benefits of Aerobic exercise eg brisk walking, backed by scientific research -

- Strengthens respiratory muscles.
- Strengthens heart muscle and lowers resting heart rate.
- Tones muscles throughout our body.
- Reduces blood pressure.
- Improves circulation.
- Raises the number of red blood cells, which improves oxygen supply and transport to all parts of body
- Sleep quality improves with moderate exercise.
- Improves mental sharpness.
- It may also reduce migraine symptoms.
- Reduces the risk of heart disease and strokes.
- Helps improve survival rates of patients with cardiovascular diseases.
- High impact aerobic exercise stimulates bone growth and reduces the risk of osteoporosis or weak bones.
- Increases stamina.
- Increases blood flow through muscles.
- Increases longevity.

Practical action steps you can implement

1. Remember *why* you started in the first place eg health issue, to stay fit, keep in shape etc- this will help keep you motivated.

2. Make time - Always include at least 1 minute of exercise per day to start within your daily grind. Yes, only 1 minute. Say to yourself "I deserve my breakfast because of my workout." "If I can't carve out 1 minute of 1440 minutes in a day, perhaps I don't deserve a breakfast." I know it sounds quite extreme, but we humans are not designed to sit at a desk all day.
3. Gradually, increase your duration from 1 to 10 to 30 minutes and so on and also the intensity of your workout.
4. Make it fun- You can only maintain a habit, you genuinely enjoy. Hence if you don't like going to the gym, relish a brisk walk or a jog. If you can't walk briskly eg due to medical reasons e.g. arthritis- do swimming. If you don't know how to swim- learn it. There are simply no excuses.
5. Find a friend to go with. Pick a partner who is committed to their health. You can socialize, have fun and also they can cheer you up when your motivation levels are low. It works both ways.
6. Make SMARTER goals - which means specific, measurable, achievable, realistic, timebound, exciting and rewarding.
7. The longer you keep it up, the longer you will continue - after a few weeks, your exercise routine soon becomes a habit. Research suggests that it takes 6-10 weeks to form a new habit- so persevere.
8. Set fitness goals. Set goals to beat your own record eg- the distance ran, push-ups or chin-ups you do, weights you lift or the number of skipping ropes.
9. Challenge your comfort zone - Your competition today is only against your best self yesterday. Not against your friend or any other person on the planet. This is the only valid and accurate comparison. If you are improving, you are growing.

10. Experiment. Mix it up and try different activities. There are many different fitness regimes you can follow or activities to try. If you don't like lifting weights or running, try sports, martial arts or dancing eg Zumba.
11. Music can enhance a workout. It adds fun and can be highly inspiring to your workout.
12. Reward yourself for exercise is rewarding your commitment to health.
13. Exercise relieves stress. We release positive hormones called endorphins when we do a workout. Having a stressful day at work means that exercise is even more important on that day. Make sure you schedule it.
14. Record achievements – eg weight loss or muscle gain is a good idea for beginners. Fitness does improve if we persevere. Investing in a personal trainer is the next step forward.
15. Walk instead of using a car or a bike. Traffic experts around the world say that the majority of car trips are very short.
16. If you are using public transport, get off at an earlier stop and walk the rest of the way. If you want to go upstairs, walk rather than taking the elevator or escalators.
17. Go for a brisk 30-minute walk five times each week. If you can't, two 15-minute sessions are equally good.
18. During your lunch break at work, go for a walk.
19. Join an exercise class eg- Zumba, Yoga, Pilates.
20. If you do housework, do it a bit more vigorously and turn it into an exercise session.

One must remember that the secret is "little and often." A little bit everyday is great - one big session once a week is not. Make sure your progress is gradual and sustained. Ensure you drink plenty of water before, during and after exercise. Check with your local doctor if you are not sure about your health. Exercise may seem like a drag, but the more you do, the easier it will become. The benefits of regular physical activity are wide-reaching and well worth making an effort for. You are much more likely to prevent modern day diseases like diabetes, high blood pressure, obesity, heart problems, strokes, etc. The list is endless. In fact, if you are on multiple medications for these ailments - adopting a healthy lifestyle will help you cut down your pills. See your local GP and discuss.

Reading → MASTERS

"Books are the quietest and most constant of friends;
they are the most accessible and wisest of counselors,
and the most patient of teachers."
— *Charles W. Eliot*

"It is what you read when you don't have to that
determines what you will be when you can't help it."
— *Oscar Wilde*

"Some books should be tasted, some devoured,
but only a few should be chewed and digested thoroughly."
— *Sir Francis Bacon*

"Books are the plane, and the train, and the road.
They are the destination, and the journey. They are home."
— *Anna Quindlen*

"A short story is a different thing altogether –
a short story is like a quick kiss in the dark from a stranger."
— *Stephen King*

Real books are real. You can feel them, smell them. Immerse yourself in them. Although more people today are buying ebooks, we can't really feel the same joy of a good, old-fashioned read like a good-old friend. We have evolved from our ancestors over a period of 5-7 million years.

The advancement of latest technology -internet and computers is only 30- 40 years old, which is negligible in evolutionary terms. Our body and minds are therefore shaped by our primal instincts. I am not a critic of technology by any means, yet I wish to emphasize that our learning tools are still inherently moulded by our evolution. Our ancestors used to make sounds, communicate with their family, paint, draw, read and write. The reading was done with the eyes and fingers (touch) and the same goes with writing. This is hard-wired in our brains and we can not remove this even if we want to. Hence it is always a good idea to invest in a real physical book. Here are some of the great benefits of reading books in general.

1. **Enriches our vocabulary**
   Diving into a good book opens up a whole world of knowledge starting from a very young age. Children's books expose kids to 40-50% more words than TV and the same applies to a chat between college graduates. This not only leads to higher scores on reading tests, but also higher scores on general intelligence tests. Plus, stronger early reading skills may mean higher intelligence later in life. Research suggests that reading on a screen can slow us down by as much as 20 to 30 percent.

2. **Boost our brain power.**
   Regular reading makes us smarter and can increase our brain power. Just like a jog exercises our heart and muscles, reading regularly improves memory by giving our brain a good workout. With age comes a decline in memory and brain function. Regular reading may help slow the process, keeping minds sharper longer, according to research published in Neurology.

3. **Reading can make us more empathetic.**
   Getting lost in a good read makes us easier to relate to others. Fiction stories have the power to help readers understand what others are thinking by reading other people's emotions, according to research published in Science. "Understanding others" is a crucial skill that enables the complex social relationships that characterize human societies.

4. **Flipping pages help us understand better.**
   The feel of paper pages under our fingertips provides our brain with some context, which directs deeper and better comprehension of the subject.

5. **Helps combat Alzheimer's disease**
   Reading puts our brain to work, and that's really cool. Those who engage their brains via activities eg- reading, chess, or puzzles can be 2.5 times less likely to develop Alzheimer's disease than those who involve in less stimulating activities. Exercising the brain may help as inactivity increases the risk of developing Alzheimer's.

6. **Reading helps us relax.**
   Research suggests that reading can work as a serious stress-killer. A 2009 study by Sussex University researchers showed that reading just for 6 minutes may reduce stress by as much as 68%. "Losing yourself in the book is the ultimate relaxation. It really doesn't matter what book you read, by losing yourself in a thoroughly engrossing book you can escape from the worries and stresses of the everyday world and spend a while exploring the domain of the author's imagination," as per cognitive neuropsychologist Dr. Lewis.

7. **Reading before bed can help us sleep better.**
   Creating a bedtime ritual eg- reading before bed, signals our body to wind down and go to sleep. Reading a real book helps us relax more than zoning out in front of a screen. Screens like e-readers and tablets can keep us awake longer and even hurt our sleep. It applies to kids too - 54% of children sleep near a small screen, and get 20 fewer minutes of sleep on an average because of it.

8. **Helps develop stronger thinking skills whether fiction or nonfiction books.**

9. **Improves Focus and Concentration**
   In our internet-addicted world, attention is disrupted as we multitask. Multitasking is a myth. We may feel more productive, but none of the work is done with full attention and good quality. When we read a book, all of our attention is focused on the story—the rest of the world just fades. We immerse ourselves in fine details. Try reading for 15-20 minutes before work eg- on your morning commute on public transport, and you'll be surprised at how much more focused you are once you get to the office.

Practical tips and action steps

1. Highlight the text with a marker pen. You may underline the important points or circle crucial words.
2. Give stars to important principles. Use your scale eg 1- 7 stars. If I am discovering something new, relevant and keen to apply immediately- I will write 7 stars. This tool is helpful as it signals our brain the importance and we register it immediately.

3. Re-read the chapter before you move to the next one. For a reader, it is always tempting to move to the next chapter as it is fresh and we want to finish the book. The problem with this approach is that we miss the highlighted starred points in the previous chapter. You will be surprised, as it may only take a few minutes depending upon the highlighted section and speed of reading, yet it is really worth our time.
4. Make diagrams, flow chart or a picture. It helps us retain the information we have gathered in our own unique way.
5. Make your own formulas as it helps us absorb the facts in a way we prefer and learn.
6. Create your own sacred reading space. Fill it up with inspiring quotes.
7. Keep your tools handy- pen, pencil, highlighter, ruler etc.
8. Take a break after a 45 minute session. Have a chat with loved ones or have a cuppa and get back to your project. We only have so much of mental energy, so rejuvenate before your next session.

Scribble → MASTERS

"Either write something worth reading or
do something worth writing."
— Benjamin Franklin

"No one can tell your story so tell it yourself.
No one can write your story so write it yourself."

"I am a writer and I will write what I want to write."
— J.K. Rowling

"The beautiful part of writing is that you don't have to
get it right the first time, unlike, say, a brain surgeon."
— Robert Cormier

"If you want to be a writer, you must do two things
above all others: read a lot and write a lot."
— Stephen King

"Reading is like breathing in,
Writing is like breathing out."
— Pam Allyn

"There is something delicious about writing
the first words of a story. You never quite know
where they'll take you."
— Beatrix Potter

Personal and non-fiction writing is a great habit, as so many successful people are admirably regular writers.

- Warren Buffet has described writing as a key way of refining his thoughts.
- Richard Branson once said "my most essential possession is a standard-sized school notebook,"
- Bill Gates has described writing as a way to sit down and re-evaluate his thoughts during the day.

Benefits of writing

1. Clear writing signals clarity. It makes us understand ourselves better. It cuts all complexity and just reveals the simple real you. We act in our own authentic genuine self.
2. Clarity through our writing breeds trust in others. When we have clarity of thoughts, it is reflected in our writing and actions, making us more reliable.
3. Writing eliminates stress. We may have hundreds of thoughts troubling us in day to day life. Jotting down these thoughts on a notebook with a pen is one of the best strategies to understand them and how they are linked to each other. Once the thought comes to paper, we have solved half of the problem. We have acknowledged the thought and now our subconscious mind is already working to find the solution.
4. Writing daily tasks is a great way of getting things done. Prioritizing those tasks is the next step. Actioning them is the vital and most crucial of all steps. Our most important tasks should always be meticulously handwritten. It is a silent yet powerful message to our subconscious minds- "Do me first. I am important." Why am I so passionate

about handwriting? It all boils down to our evolution. We are designed over a million yrs to handwrite, draw art and that's how our brain naturally learns and engages. The technological advances made are great, yet does not serve us well in this ancient skill of *learning via handwriting*.
5. Writing short term, medium and long term goals is another great quadrant 2 activity. We act on them once we have clarity and writing is the best tool to achieve them.
6. Writing the synopsis or key points of a subject is another great skill. It helps us to remember the crucial concepts and more importantly why. Hence, we are more likely to act on our learning.
7. Since a simple act of writing our thoughts leads to clarity, it helps us in better decision making in all aspects of our lives.
8. Writing our thoughts out makes us more focused and our dreams come true as we have full conviction, dedication and moving in the right direction.

Practical Action steps -

All the above quotes are related to writing your own story or blogs or perhaps books. The good news is that it is applicable to our daily lives and not just books. So exactly, what can you write? There are many wide-ranging options -

1. Your daily to-do list. Yes, it is important. When we make a habit of making it and action them, we feel happy and accomplished. It is a good idea to include our most urgent as well as the most important activities for that day. (examples on page 47)

2. Then comes our medium term goals eg- those we wish to achieve in 3-6 months time. Eg learning a new hobby, sports, language or adopting a new lifestyle. These can be categorized into weekly and then daily goals. The idea is similar to slicing a big elephant into smaller parts which is relatively easier to do and doesn't look so monumental. Write.
3. Finally comes our long term goals which are based on our true *Why*. Writing is an outlet to know ourselves better, to understand who we are and the direction we are going. Are we going in the right direction? Write.
4. Writing helps us define our goals, core values and true calling with utmost clarity. A written word is embedded in our brain. When I say write, it means written on a physical paper and not on any screen. It boils down to finger, hand and brain coordination and learning via an old fashioned way, we are hardwired to. Over a period of last 10-15 years, I have tried both types of writing on paper and screen. I always *recall* the paper version better. From evolutionary terms, it makes sense not to ignore this powerful practice.
5. Investing in a good journal is a good idea. It only becomes great when you start writing. Practice daily.
6. Write at least a few minutes every day. It will soon become a good habit.
7. Keep it with you most of the times so you capture any fresh ideas or eureka moments coming to mind.
8. Write 5 gratefulness sentences every morning, a beautiful sacred practice to start your day.
9. I usually prefer a dated journal which is helpful when tracking what I have written a couple of months ago.

10. In simple terms a *written plan* or goals leads to *clarity*. This should be followed by *consistent daily small actions*. It soon becomes our *daily friend* or habit and leads to *Mastery* over a course of months or years.
11. Write down your goals on an index card or create a list of goals on your digital devices, then read these goals everyday. It is a great way to remind our sub-conscious brain. Read your written goals 10-30 times per day. Sir Richard Branson, a living legend, believes that millionares read their goals 1-17 times per day and billionares read their goals 19-29 times per day. Sir Richard personally reads his goals on an average 21 times each day.
12. Once we practiced the habit long enough and covered the points 1-11, we can move on to advanced levels and write poems, short stories, blogs, articles and even books.

Story Sharing → MASTERS

"Owning your story is the bravest thing you will ever do."
—Brene Brown

"There is no greater agony than bearing
an untold story inside you. What is your story?"
— Maya Angelou

"Step out of the history that is holding you back.
Step into the new story that you are willing to create."
— Oprah Winfrey

"Words are how we think; stories are how we link."
— Christina Baldwin

"Story allows our imperfections to be set in a context
that shows we are still good people."
— Annette Simmons

"Storytelling is the most powerful way to
put ideas into the world."
— Robert McKee

"Write your story as it needs to be written.
Write it honestly, and tell it as best you can. I'm not sure
there are any other rules. Not ones that matter."
— Neil Gaiman

> "When you stand and share your story in an empowering way, your story will heal you and your story will heal someone else."
>
> — Iyanla Vanzant

> "If you don't turn your life into a story, you just become a part of someone else's story."
>
> — Terry Pratchett

Before the era of paper and printing, knowledge and wisdom were passsed down generation to generation, largely in the form of stories. It's a natural part of the human evolution and hence it is such a strong learning tool. Here are the benefits of this ancient art-

1. Stories help us truly engage and connect with our audience.
2. Authentic engagement with stories releases natural hormones in our body like cortisol and oxytocin. When we are truly immersed in a story and there is tension building up, we release cortisol which is a natural fight or flight hormone and oxytocin when we are feeling compassionate.
3. A story shared in a powerful way means that we have shared our values and belief system with our audience. They are touched and make an inspired action. In some ways, it transforms them.
4. We remember stories better than any other type of information. Scientists have many reasons, but the main reason is that stories engage our brain much powerfully than logic and facts. E.g. memory champions create story versions to memorize the order of 52 cards in a deck in under 20 seconds. They craft a variation of the story based on the order of the cards, and they use this story for recall.

Practical action steps for you

1. We all have a story to tell. Our most powerful stories are the ones with mistakes, adversities and challenges. These simple, ordinary stories resonate and relate with our audience to think... "*I had a similar experience too...*" Practice sharing your stories with your loved ones, friends, staff and in fact anyone.
2. Our audience connects with us deeply when we share our true authentic self with them. This breeds mutual trust and it is more likely to influence their behaviour and empower them to take action.
3. We like facts and logic only to some extent, but, love stories as we feel them.
4. Our story is a gift to others. Our team benefits by knowing our perspective from their lens. They learn from our mistakes and ultimately inspire them.
5. There is a story in our everyday life happening right *now*. We should be ready to capture it via notebook, photos, videos and voice recorder. Replaying help understand ourselves better. When we share it with our loved ones or team in a business setting, it gives us context to share our viewpoint.
6. We are also able to connect the dots of our past stories and find meaning in them. Our audience love them, as they can relate.
7. All stories require us to be mindful. To be really present and engaging with our team. Having deep meaningful conversations. We should listen with full attention. Sometimes, there is a conversation in the unspoken word- just pure emotion.

8. There is no such thing as a good or bad story. The only thing which matter is, whether it is relevant in a particular context or not. A story which may be completely out of sync in one setting, might be highly inspiring in another situation.
9. Stories sharing our own vulnerability are the most powerful ones eg Ted talk by Brene Brown and Monica Lewinsky. So share it, bring to the world. The idea is not to glorify self but to empower others to take an inspired action.

Practising MASTERS in daily life

By now, you have gone through all the stories and MASTERS. The reality is that none of this work or principles matter, if you don't practise it. Every thought, idea, facts, knowledge is fruitless unless acted upon. Hence I will go through practical strategies that you can apply in your life. The idea is to empower you to a more happier and miraculous you. Your competition is always going to be with your past self. If you are better than your previous self couple of months ago, then surely you are a winner in your eyes and it is really the most important feeling in your life. It doesn't matter what others think of you. Yes, it surely does matter a huge lot what you think about yourself. So with this mindset, I will go through some practical tips. Again, these are only one way of doing it. Please feel free to modify them as per your unique needs.

1. MASTERS start with M and I wish to emphasize the importance of meditation first thing in the morning everyday. It really does impact, how you start your day with. Just doing 10 minutes of meditation exercise is highly beneficial to our soul. If you can not do 10 minutes, please do 5 minutes. If you can not do 5 minutes, start with just 1 minute. Essentially what I am implying is - there is no excuse for not doing it.

2. Carve out time during mini-breaks, mid-morning and late afternoon and you can practice mindfulness and meditation exercises. Again, even 1 minute of these exercises throughout the day have a compounding effect.
3. Positive affirmations are best done in the morning. You can say it silently in your mind during your commute. It is best to visualize achieving them when you are saying to self. Most importantly, these affirmations work only if you act on them as the formula is PA = 3P x A.
4. I usually say it loud with my son and daughter during our daily commute to school. The benefit is therefore also passed on to my kids. You can apply the same in your life and the practice can be done with your loved ones.
5. Smiling is contagious and makes you happy, nice and kind. It makes the receiver of your smile happy as well. It is a win-win habit. Practice it and ensure that you make at least 5 people smile every day. If you have a bad day at work- smile at yourself-ultimately you are a human, not a robot and can make unintentional mistakes at times.
6. Write "Make your smiles count" on your computer, laptop, phone, bathroom mirror, door etc. Ensure, you smile as you see it everyday and soon it becomes a great valuable asset to you and loved ones.
7. Practice silence in the morning as it is a great habit to help us reflect and introspect. Just 5 minutes per day on your own gives so many key ideas and fresh insights. These unique perspectives are always there in the background and silence help us tap into our subconscious minds. Practice going away from your desk during the mid-day break, eg- walking silently to a park serves both meditation and silence.

8. Practice silence and active listening when communicating. It is the most powerful yet vastly underutilized communication tool on our planet.
9. Thinking and reflecting go hand in hand with silence. We can only do a meaningful introspection of ourselves when quiet. Writing our thoughts on a journal is a great way of knowing self. So invest in a journal, keep it with you at all times and most importantly write.
10. Thanking or gratitude is one of the most important habits of champions. Make sure you cultivate it. Practice it by saying a short prayer every day or you can write 5 small simple sentences of gratefulness to loved ones or anyone, anywhere. You can write in your gratitude journal. Practice saying "Thank you" politely, kindly with gratefulness genuinely reflecting from your tone and body language.
11. Physical Exercise is a vital aspect of our well being. It's usually a good idea to devote at least 30 mins/day - 5 days a week. For beginners, start with 5 mins/day and gradually build on. Consistency is highly important and it is far better to do seven 10 minute sessions per week, compared to one big 60-minute session on a weekend. Ensure you get a bit puffed up when exercising.
12. Cultivate the habit of daily reading- books you enjoy and even something new unexplored territory. Like other habits, a routine of regular reading is the key. It is a good idea to devote 10-20 minutes of reading per day. For beginners, a 5 minute spell of reading is a great starting point to build on. If you can not read on weekdays, ensure you schedule some quality reading time on weekends. You will be surprised how much you have learned only in a couple of months.

13. Scribble and jot down your thoughts, as they come, in your journal. Make pictures, diagram, flow chart or formula. Everyone is unique and we have different methods of learning. Writing your thoughts in a gratitude journal is a great starting point. Start today.
14. Study the art of story sharing. Practice it. It is one of the most beautiful habits you can learn and influence your loved ones at home, work or any other setting. A short story delivered in an appropriate context is one of the most powerful ways you can win the love of your family and friends.

Final thoughts on MASTERS

"Consistent, focused and deliberate practice of MASTERS is the key action to achieve the mastery of your life."

"We are what we repeatedly do.
Excellence, then, is not an act, but a habit."
— *Aristotle*

"Practice without theory is more valuable than a theory without practice."
— *Marcus Quintilianus*

"Excellence is not a gift, but a skill that takes practice.
We do not act rightly because we are excellent,
In fact we achieve excellence by acting rightly."
— *Plato*

"Practice daily, because the quality of your practice determines the calibre of your performance."
— *Robin Sharma*

"Success has to do with deliberate practice.
Practice must be focused, determined, and in an environment where there's feedback."
— *Malcolm Gladwell*

"Practice like you've never won,
Perform like you've never lost."
— *Bernard F. Asuncion*

References

1. https://www.entrepreneur.com/article/297833- Combating the Millennial Attention Span to Keep Your Team Engaged
2. Authentic Happiness- using the new positive psychology to realize your potential for lasting fulfillment- Martin.E.P. Seligman
3. The 7 habits of highly effective people- Stephen. R. Covey
4. https://www.thebetterindia.com/126209/dadi-ki-rasoi-meals-rs5/
5. https://un.org.au/2014/05/14/who-hunger-statistics/
6. https://www.buzzfeed.com/worldhumanitarianday/world-humanitarian-day
7. https://www.facebook.com/swapnaugustine/
8. https://english.manoramaonline.com/women/on-a-roll/2018/03/19/born-armless-swapna-augustine-artist.html
9. https://www.terryfox.org/
10. https://en.wikipedia.org/wiki/Terry_Fox
11. http://www.ldsliving.com/Let-It-Go-A-Story-of-Tragedy-and-the-Power-of-Forgiveness/s/71058
12. https://www.theguardian.com/technology/2017/apr/30/google-mo-gawdat-solve-for-happy-interview
13. https://www.jackcanfield.com/blog/affirmations/
14. https://www.forbes.com/sites/ericsavitz/2011/03/22/the-untapped-power-of-smiling/#5ae713a87a67
15. https://www.huffpost.com/entry/happiness-tips_n_5153819
16. http://www.bbc.com/future/story/20170407-why-all-smiles-are-not-the-same
17. https://www.lifehack.org/377243/science-says-silence-much-more-important-our-brains-than-thought

18. www.psychologytoday.com/blog/the-moment-youth/201312/the-importance-silence-in-noisy-world
19. www.medicaldaily.com/5-health-benefits-being-silent-your-mind-and-body-396934
20. top7business.com/?Enjoy-The-Silence:-The-7-Powers-of-Silence&id=716
21. www.huffingtonpost.com/entry/silence-brain-benefits_us_56d83967e4b0000de4037004
22. Woronko, M(n.d) The power of self-reflection. Ten questions you should ask yourself. https://www.lifehack.org/articles/communication/you-want-happy-you-need-ask-yourself-these-10-questions-every-morning.html
23. William, D.k (n.d)30 thought provoking questions you should ask yourself every day.
24. Positive Psychology Progress (2005, Seligman, M. P., Steen, T. A., Park, N., & Peterson, C.)
25. Counting Blessings Versus Burdens: An Experimental Investigation of Gratitude and Subjective Well-Being in Daily Life
26. Gratitude Uniquely Predicts Satisfaction with Life: Incremental Validity Above the Domains and Facets of the Five Factor Model
27. Sacks, D. W., Stevenson, B., & Wolfers, J. (2012). The new stylized facts about income and subjective well-being. Emotion, 12(6), 1181.
28. The Role of Gratitude in The Development of Social Support, Stress, and Depression: Two Longitudinal Studies
29. Why Gratitude Enhances Well-Being: What We Know, What We Need to Know
30. Stone, D. I., & Stone, E. F. (1983). The Effects of Feedback Favorability and Feedback Consistency. Academy of Management Proceedings (00650668), 178-182. doi:10.5465/AMBPP.1983.4976341
31. Coping Style as a Psychological Resource of Grateful People
32. C. Peterson, L. Bossio. "Optimism and Physical Wellbeing." Optimism & Pessimism: Implications for Theory, Research, and Practice. Ed. E. Chang. Washington, DC: American Psychological Association, 2001: 127-145.
33. Positive Emotions in Early Life and Longevity: Findings from The Nun Study
34. Optimists vs. Pessimists Survival Rate Among Medical Patients Over a 30-Year Period

35. Kashdan, T. B., & Breen, W. E. (2007). Materialism and diminished well being: experiential avoidance as a mediating mechanism. Journal of Social & Clinical Psychology, 26(5), 521-539.
36. Belk, R. W. (1985). Materialism: Trait aspects of living in the material world. Journal of Consumer Research, 12, 265 – 280
37. Stanton A, Snider P. Coping with a breast cancer diagnosis: A prospective study. Health Psychol. 1993; 12(1): 16–23 [serial online].
38. Segerstrom S, Taylor S, Kemeny M, Fahey J. Optimism is associated with mood, coping and immune change in response to stress. J Pers Soc Psychol. 1998; 74(6): 1646–1655 [serial online].
39. Gratitude: Effects on Perspective and Blood Pressure (2007)
40. http://onlinelibrary.wiley.com/doi/10.1111/cdev.12272/full
41. http://www.sciencedaily.com/releases/2014/07/140724094209.htm
42. https://www.ischool.utexas.edu/~adillon/Journals/Reading.htm (0.8)
43. https://n.neurology.org/content/81/4/314. (1)
44. http://www.sciencemag.org/content/342/6156/377.abstract. (2)
45. http://www.wired.com/2014/05/reading-on-screen-versus-paper/ (3)
46. http://www.pnas.org/content/98/6/3440.full (4)
47. http://www.kumon.co.uk/blog/reading-reduces-stress-levels/ (5)
48. http://www.mayoclinic.org/healthy-living/adult-health/in-depth/sleep/art-20048379 (6)
49. http://www.vox.com/2014/12/22/7435685/ipad-sleep (7)
50. http://pediatrics.aappublications.org/content/early/2015/01/01/peds.2014-2306.abstract (8)
51. https://journals.sagepub.com/doi/abs/10.1177/0146167201277003
52. https://www.psychologytoday.com/intl/basics/dreaming
53. http://psycnet.apa.org/journals/psp/84/2/377/
54. https://www.wirebuzz.com/benefits-of-storytelling/

Acknowledgments

Foremost, I am utmost grateful to the challenges encountered in the first half of my life. I believe I am in a position to write this book because of them. My loving parents have always blessed me with their unconditional love and support which shaped me profoundly. I have been blessed to have a loving extended family and friends who have always showered me with their blessings.

I am immensely grateful to the thousands of encounters with my patients, my clients, who have always been a source of inspiration to me. The challenges they encounter in their lives that they share with me always remind me of the unique resilience of mankind, and how we can learn from them using a positive frame of mind.

I am thankful to my editor Mr. Simon Richardson for giving me useful insights and feedback. I am highly appreciative of the useful advice and countless conversations with our publisher Mr. William Webster and his team in regards to the final layout of this book.

I have a deep sense of respect and gratitude to all my teachers who have been my lighthouse. I have not seen a significant proportion of my teachers as they are either not physically alive today or reside in different countries. However, their teachings and pearls of wisdom always reside in my heart. Their guidance via books, audio-tapes and conversations have transformed me profoundly, and I continue to learn this way.

Finally, I am grateful to the tightly knit group of close friends who have always supported the cause which was my purpose for writing this book. Last, but not least, I am utmost blessed to have a beautiful relationship with my loving wife and soul-mate Priyanka who supported me during all tough challenging times, trials and tribulations. My two beautiful loving kids Molly and Megh have always been a beacon of light to us and give me inspiring ideas to bring out the best in myself. We are a very close knit family team who support each other at all times. Together we can achieve more and make our world a beautiful place to live.

www.ingramcontent.com/pod-product-compliance
Lightning Source LLC
Chambersburg PA
CBHW071459080526
44587CB00014B/2159